Praise

'A step-by-step guide to help ι
our money. This easy-to-follow book will give us all
a simple toolkit to make our money go further, feel
more in control and build security and freedom.'
   — **Holly Mackay**, Founder and CEO of
      Boring Money

'The secret to a future of financial freedom is to break
bad money habits and develop better ones. In this
book, Rob shows you how.'
   — **Mike Harris**, Founder of First Direct
      and Egg

'In an easy-to-read way, you can follow the steps to
form good money habits that will transform your
financial freedom and the future prosperity of the
planet. Reading and sharing this book is important in
breaking the stigma attached to talking about money
with friends, family and future generations.'
   — **Dr Daniel Crosby**, author and behavioural
      finance expert

'This book isn't a get-rich-quick manual – it's much more than that. Rob helps the reader build the deep knowledge and sustainable habits that are the bedrock of a healthy relationship with money. Read, learn and prosper!'
— **Iona Bain**, author of OWN IT, i-columnist, speaker and broadcaster specialising in young finances

'Robert is the master of money. This book shares the real wisdom you wish you had known sooner. The ideas are simple and sustainable. Follow his three steps to create financial stability and abundance for the long term.'
— **Daniel Priestley**, author of *The Entrepreneur Revolution*

Three money moves to transform your finances

FREEDOM

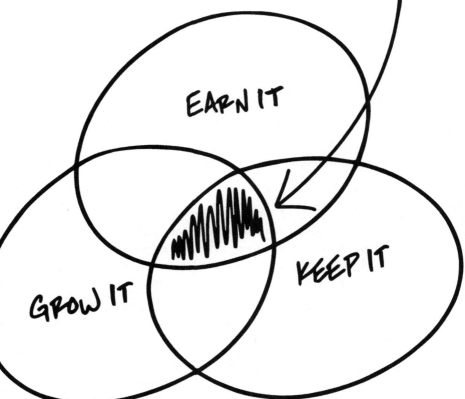

EARN IT

GROW IT

KEEP IT

ROBERT GARDNER

ILLUSTRATED BY CARL RICHARDS

R^ethink

First published in Great Britain in 2023 by Rethink Press (www.rethinkpress.com)

Cover image and illustrations by Carl Richards

Contents

Disclaimer

I hope you enjoy reading the book and find it informative and easy to read. Please do your own research or seek financial advice before making financial decisions or investing any money. Nothing in this book should be considered investment advice.

The information in the book is up-to-date as of early 2023.

Preface

Where I'm coming from

My name's Rob Gardner, and I'm passionate about empowering people to achieve financial freedom in a world worth living in. I am focused on making money a force for good for the planet and those who live on it.

I've worked in financial services for over twenty years, mainly specialising in pensions. I love pensions – not only their power to transform everyone's financial future, but their potential to transform the future prosperity of the planet. I have built two B-Corp businesses. In 2006 I co-founded Redington, a leading investment and pensions consultancy, to create financial wellbeing for 100 million people in a way that secures and protects the planet's future, and in 2009 I co-founded Mallowstreet, an online pension community whose purpose is to deliver a better retirement for everyone. RedSTART, a financial education charity that transforms the life chances of some of the UK's most disadvantaged children was born in 2012. Our ambition is to change the game and give every child a financial education that counts.

I have dedicated myself to helping people to understand how money works and how to make money work for them. Everyone has the right to financial freedom, and most of us have the means to achieve it. It begins with awareness of your situation with money, then understanding your relationship with money to build the confidence to make better decisions around keeping and growing what you are already earning.

While preparing for this book, I spoke to a diverse range of people and found that many are making the same financial mistakes. This is not due to a lack of care but because they need to have the right kind of financial knowledge and guidance. For many of us, talking about money is a taboo subject. We are not taught about money in school and often don't learn it from our parents. It's no wonder our financial literacy levels are so low. As the father of two young girls, we must make talking about money part of our daily conversations. Doing so can break the debt cycle and low financial literacy levels for future generations.

My aim is to help you understand money and make better financial decisions. Your journey to financial freedom is about more than how much you earn. It's about how much you keep and grow. It's about doing a few simple things consistently for a long time. These habits will empower you to understand how money works, and how to make money work for you.

I also want you to understand the incredible impact your money can have as a force for good on the planet. This way, the next generation enjoys financial freedom and a world worth living in because, beyond your financial freedom, this book has a bigger purpose. It's about using your money as a force for good. By choosing how you grow your money, you can address some of the most significant issues we face today, ranging from climate change to social inequality. I promise you that by spending just a few minutes a day reading my book, you will begin to think differently about money. You will also be more confident about making financial decisions and know when to seek help or further advice.

Please note I am British and live and work in the UK, so all worked examples are based on UK figures and GBP (£), but the shared concepts and tools offered can be applied globally. To simplify, I rounded figures and calculations to whole numbers. For example, £29,000 has been rounded to £30,000 or 87% to nine out of ten.

Chapter overview

1. **Let's talk about money:** We'll start with talking about and understanding your relationship with money. This is one of the best things you can do to help yourself, your family and future generations achieve financial freedom.

Part One: Earn It

2. **It's not what you earn, it's what you do with it that counts:** In this chapter, you'll learn to mind your money business and not forsake your financial health to keep up appearances. Just because someone looks wealthy doesn't mean that they are. Learn how to set goals and form sustainable habits – money habits, which will allow you to focus on yourself and decide how you can, or want to, earn your money.

3. **Understanding your payslip:** It may sound simple (or even dull) but getting to know your payslip (think of it as your financial Fitbit) is the key to your financial freedom by tracking how much you're earning and keeping.

4. **Become more valuable:** Building financial freedom is much easier when earning £60,000 a year rather than £30,000. This chapter will look at six strategies to help you become more valuable by increasing your earning potential.

Part Two: Keep It

5. **Building your financial resilience:** Your journey to financial freedom starts with learning how to save for your rainy-day fund. Emergency savings are like smartphones – we all need them but letting them run to low-battery mode leaves us feeling anxious and vulnerable. Small but consistent saving habits help you build financial resilience.

6. **Weatherproofing your finances:** Unfortunately, financial storms can affect us anytime and from any direction. Your savings, habits and financial decisions give you the resilience you need to cope with the bad weather and allow you to enjoy the sunshine that follows the storm.

7. **Tax wrappers matter:** It might surprise you to know that the government wants you to save money. There are several tax wrappers and investment accounts to help you, which you may need to be aware of. Once you understand which tax wrappers are suitable for you, I'll show you how to use them to get the deposit for a house in ten years.

Part Three: Grow It

8. **Meet your future self:** When it comes to growing your money for your future financial freedom, it's important to remember you're not saving for something abstract. What you're keeping is for

you. You are putting money away for your future self – and you'll thank yourself for it later.

9. **Calculate your net worth:** I'll teach you that being 'rich' is an appearance. Building your net worth is the only way to be truly financially free.

10. **Compounding matters – get interested:** In this chapter, we'll look at one of the most impactful concepts in money – compound interest. I'll show you how, with a bit of patience, it can impact your savings by investing for decades, not days.

11. **In it to win it:** The most challenging part about investing is getting started. The second and most demanding part is staying put. So when it comes to achieving financial freedom through investing, I'll share the mythological story of Ulysses, which teaches us how to ignore the Sirens (the alarming headlines) and invest for the long run.

12. **Diversify:** Here, you'll learn that to achieve financial freedom, it pays to diversify your investments and invest for the long term rather than as a speculator bouncing from one trend to the next.

13. **Invest responsibly:** Suppose enough of us invest in the right way. In that case, we can be on the right side of climate history and help change the shape of the economy from linear to circular.

14. **Your money as a force for good:** Where you earn your money, where you save, where you

spend your money and invest your money all impact the world. Save for your future self and the future of the planet.

15. **The crypto conundrum:** The digital asset universe is broad, and the opinions surrounding it are even more expansive. Invest time in learning about this world before you invest your money.

16. **Can crypto be a force for good?** Bitcoin, the original digital money, is known for its high energy use. Still, not all digital assets are significant energy users. In this chapter, we explore what it takes to make sure your crypto is mined responsibly.

Part Four: Preserve It

17. **Alpine descent:** Good financial planning doesn't stop when it comes to enjoying your retirement. You've worked hard to get there – but here I'll show you how to maintain financial resilience throughout your retirement, having a plan and considering financial advice so that you can make your pension last.

18. **How to leave a financial legacy:** Empower others to achieve financial resilience by sharing the lessons of this book. You will be paying it forward by speaking about money with just a couple of people. This is because normalising conversations about money has a broader impact than you may think.

1

Let's Talk About Money

'An investment in knowledge pays the best interest.'
— Benjamin Franklin, a Nobel Prize
winner for his work on financial theory

Today, many of us are living longer and healthier lives, which is something to be celebrated. *Living long* is one thing, but to *prosper*, our wealth, like our health, needs to be prioritised. We need to plan carefully, and save little and often, to ensure we have enough money to live within our means for a long time after we retire.

We need to understand our relationship with money to realise how it may be harming or helping our future financial freedom. We should speak regularly with those we trust about our financial plans, to ensure we're on track to meet them, but, in the UK, money is a taboo subject. In fact, research tells us that parents would rather talk to their children about sex than money, and that a quarter of UK adults would rather talk about almost *anything* else – infidelity, abortion, parenting techniques – than their finances (Dunn, 2016).

It's a cycle we need to break, because it results in many adults not understanding the basics of money management, nor how to build up their *financial resilience*. Being unable to deal with setbacks can seriously impact our day-to-day lives and mental health. What's more, not talking about money means we're not helping our children and grandchildren to become financially literate. With future generations increasingly likely to live to the age of 100, this is a huge long-term problem if we have any hope for our children and grandchildren prospering later in life (DWP, 2010).

Take a moment to think about how often you talk about your personal finances with your friends, parents, partner or children. Think about how often those people talk to you about money. If the answer is 'not a lot', you're in the majority. More than half of UK adults fear that they might be judged if they express money worries. A quarter of us don't like to talk about how much we earn because we think others will base our abilities on our salaries.

One in five couples worry that talking to their partner about their finances could end their relationship (Hughes, 2019). Talking about money is a common fear – not only because most of our parents never talked about money, but because no one has taught our generation how to do it. But the value of talking about money has never been greater. To face financial challenges, understand how to improve our financial situation, get advice and grow our wealth and financial wellbeing, we need to start having conversations now.

Fight the fear and start the conversation

When people ask 'How are you?', the chances are you don't mind sharing that you've had the flu or have recovered from a recent injury, but you're less likely to discuss your mental health or money worries. As with mental health challenges, bottling up financial concerns feeds anxiety. Everyone has had a money issue at some point in their life, so there will be people in your network with advice and lessons that could be useful to you, and there are plenty of places you can turn to:

- **Someone you trust:** There may be someone in your personal network you can turn to for advice. This might include a friend, a friend's parent if you can't turn to yours, or someone you are friendly with and talk to regularly on a professional basis, such as a business owner in your local area. If they don't have relevant advice, they may know someone who does.

- **Your partner:** A great way to start talking about money as a couple is to share your own concerns with your partner. A recent study showed that married people have the fewest number of conversations about money than any type of couple, including people who are cohabiting, dating or separated. Interestingly, money is also one of the most common reasons for divorce or marital strife in the UK (McCoy, 2019). If you're a married couple or in a civil partnership, getting this right could also help you to grow your wealth by 77% more than those living alone, so it's really worth talking about it and getting on the same page with your financial goals (Roberts, 2018).

- **Your employer:** Surprising as it might seem, your HR department or employer is someone you might be able to turn to. An increasing number of companies are offering financial wellbeing support because they know anxiety about money impacts mental health and how people perform at work. If your employer doesn't have a support system, ask them why not. It could prompt them to initiate one. You can even request that your employer work with a company like Salary Finance, which works with employers to offer fixed-rate loans to its employees for anything from consolidating debt to bigger-ticket items like buying a house. These are paid back by a salary deduction.

- **Social support:** If you're worried, anxious or confused about your personal finances, saying it aloud and hearing other people's stories can help be the first step towards making a change. Since the pandemic, numerous consumer-friendly personal finance blogs, apps, Instagram accounts and podcasts have launched. Dedicated to talking all things money – including debt – you can now look outside of your personal network for advice or to hear other people's experiences and what worked for them. @allourbestintentions, @boringmoney_hq, @getwokenotbroke and @moneymedics are all great accounts to help with this, and there are many more out there, so I recommend you find those that best work for you. Ultimately, when it comes to talking about money, burying your head in the sand will cost you more than your mental health, as any debts or bills left ignored will always catch up with you in the end. Opening up will help you to see that you're not alone in your money worries and that support is out there – allowing you to take the right steps towards a more confident, clearer attitude towards your finances.

Begin with the end in mind

Depending on where you are in your life, you may not have thought much about retirement and find it at the bottom of your list of financial priorities – after getting debt-free, saving for a house or a big-ticket item and paying off your mortgage.

At the time of publishing this book (mid 2023), both the cost of living and inflation are at an all-time high, many Brits are still recouping losses following the pandemic and their salaries have stagnated. On top of this, because of staggering house prices, Millennials (those born between 1981 and 1990) have been dubbed 'the avocado on toast generation', perceived as opting to enjoy life rather than take on the seemingly impossible feat of getting on the property ladder, while the stressed-out 'sandwich generation' (those responsible for both their ageing parents and their own children) are caught in the middle of their own financial burdens.

With the numerous challenges spanning generations, it's easy to understand why beginning with the end in mind and planning for your pension isn't the number one priority for most people. 'How much money do I need to retire?' is perhaps the most important question we should be asking ourselves about our finances, yet one in three Brits don't know how big a pension pot they'll need. One in five don't even know how much they have. And many underestimate how long they'll live, so risk running out of money before they die (Green, 2020).

To live long and prosper, you need to take care of your financial wellbeing now to create wealth for yourself later over a longer period. That requires saving for today, tomorrow and the day after tomorrow. It also requires investing in a responsible way. In the following chapters, I will take you through every step of the way to get you thinking long term about your finances and financial wellbeing – for which your future self will thank you for. Let's kick off your financial journey from the first step: *earning it.*

Your Financial Freedom Scorecard

To get the most out of this book, it's helpful to gain an understanding of where you are on your journey by completing the Financial Freedom' scorecard.

Go to https://yourfinancialfreedom.scoreapp.com and answer the questions. This will give you a detailed report with your baseline 'FR££DOM' score and recommendations on where and how you can make better financial decisions and achieve financial freedom. Once you have read the book and implemented some of the actions you can retake the test to monitor your progress.

PART ONE
EARN IT

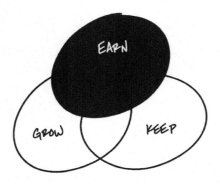

'It's not how much money you make, but how much money you keep, how hard it works for you, and how many generations you keep it for.'
— Robert Kiyosaki

2

It's Not What You Earn, It's What You Do With It That Counts

'It's not about how much you make; it's about how much you keep.'
— Shaquille O'Neal

The key to financial freedom is less about how much you earn; it's more about knowing how to keep and grow what you already have. Understanding these three key principles – *earn it, keep it, grow it* – will allow you to manage your money and make better long-term financial decisions. It's honestly that simple. Think of 'earn it, keep it, grow it' as a system of habits that will help you achieve remarkable results. James Clear says in his book *Atomic Habits: An Easy and Proven Way to Build Good Habits and Break Bad Ones*, 'A tiny change in your behaviour will not transform your life overnight. But turn that behaviour into a habit that you perform every day, and it absolutely can lead to big changes' (Clear, 2021).

In this chapter I'm going to share some stories that will illustrate how important these three components are to securing your financial wellbeing. I haven't always got it right, but if you can learn from my mistakes and start making the right financial decisions now and for your future self, then you'll be well on your way to achieving long-term wealth and prosperity.

Keeping up with the Kardashians

We're living in an age of comparison. Thanks in part to social media, as well as keeping up with the Joneses, we're now having to keep up with the Kardashians. It's reassuring to know that things aren't always as they seem through the filter of Instagram. Dr Joy Lere, a clinical psychologist and behavioural finance consultant, wrote on 'The Money Panel' blog (Lere, 2020), 'I have sat behind closed doors with the Joneses. . . It turns out – up close – the Joneses are not as rich, beautiful or happy as you thought.'

Just because someone earns a lot – or looks like they do – doesn't mean that they're automatically wealthy and financially secure. On 'Oprah's Master Class: The Podcast', Shaquille O'Neal, an NBA basketball player from the 1990s, tells the story of how, within an hour of signing his first professional basketball contract in 1992, he spent $1 million. He didn't realise there were various taxes and fees to be paid on his earnings. He probably netted $700,000, but in his mind, he had $1 million to spend.

He started with buying a new car. 'I always wanted a black-on-black Mercedes-Benz,' Shaq said. 'I go get it. Boom, $150,000.' When he gets home, his father jokingly asks, 'Where's mine?' He ends up buying one for his dad, and another for his mum. Having bought three cars, the spending didn't stop there. He bought himself diamond jewellery, new suits and fancy clothes. A few days later, his bank manager calls to show Shaq a spreadsheet with all his expenses. He tells Shaq that a lot of athletes end up with nothing when they stop playing, and says, 'You're a bright, young star. I don't want you to be like that. You need to learn how to take care and manage your money.'

This valuable life lesson in 'keeping it' was all Shaq needed to get his finances back on track.

Shaq follows his story up with brilliant budgeting advice from another mentor. The mentor took a piece of paper and wrote $100 on it. He then ripped the paper in half and told Shaq that smart people invest $50 and then they have $50 left to spend. From then on, Shaq invested 50% of his income to 'grow' for the long term. He then kept 25% in savings and spent the remaining 25% on 'fun things' like cars, houses and jewellery. He retired in 2011 and remains a wealthy man, having invested in shares, property and various business ventures.

Sadly, Shaq is in the minority when it comes to financial wellbeing. Two out of three NBA players are bankrupt five years after they stop playing professionally. Statistics for NFL players are worse: four out of five experience financial distress only two years after retirement (Torre, 2009). The challenge most professional athletes have is they make all their career earnings in a short period of time. They need to keep and grow their earnings to build long-term wealth and prosperity to last for the rest of their lives. Many high-earning professional athletes succumb to the lifestyle of being rich and famous and 'keeping up with the Joneses' by buying fancy cars, clothes and jewellery, which is financially fatal. Shaq gives this advice to new NBA players: 'This money isn't going to last forever. You've got to save it; you've got to invest it and you've got to be smart' (Elkins, 2019).

Shaq's advice doesn't only apply to professional athletes. We see this disparity time and again across many different industries. Although with the NBA in mind, you only need to compare superstar Michael Jordan with Dennis Rodman. Jordan has earned, kept and continues to grow his money, currently worth $1.7 billion (Forbes, 2022) and running rings around Rodman – who, despite retiring thirteen years later, is worth $500,000 (HITC, 2022). The difference between the two? Their financial habits.

Awareness creates change

You might feel that to be financially resilient, or to save for your future, you need to earn a hefty salary. That isn't the case. Two people could earn the same amount – for example, £30,000 a year (the average salary in the UK) – and one could be wealthy and the other poor (ONS, 2021). Making different financial decisions leads to different levels of wealth and financial wellbeing. This is true of all 'levels' of income.

Jess started working as an administrator at a university at the age of eighteen. Like a lot of people her age, she used store cards (credit cards for individual retailers) to buy new clothes and accessories from Oxford

Street in London. Jess was not alone in falling victim to the lure of store cards – they're pushed hard at new customers. The problem for Jess was that she ended up having so many store cards that when we first started working together, she was drowning in store card debt.

You might not know this, but to get a store card, you don't have to go through any credit checks or referencing. To open an individual savings account or a pension for your kids, you'll have to jump through all kinds of hoops, but Jess could walk into any high street store and be offered a store card to buy anything she wanted. She just had to pay the minimum monthly instalment and it was fine. Or so she thought. The thing they don't tell you about store cards is that their Annual Percentage Rate (APR) is typically 25% to 30% (Bridgen, 2022). This means the amount you must pay the store back is doubling every two to three years. If you spend £2,000 on clothes and shoes, then in three years' time, those items may be in the back of the wardrobe and no longer used or fashionable – but you now owe £4,000. And that just keeps growing.

Jess' financial situation came about because she was unaware of the APR. Why would she have been? The stores don't tell you, and it's often concealed in the small print in technical and legalistic language, which makes it hard to understand. What's more, as we know, no one talks about these things – so it's hardly surprising she didn't understand what she was getting herself into.

Buy now, pay later (BNPL) schemes are similar, with the likes of Klarna, Afterpay and Zilch dubbed the twenty-first-century spin on store credit. Since the Covid-19 pandemic, BNPL schemes have increased in popularity, with one in three people having used retail finance for their purchases, spending on average around £560 per year (Ross, 2020). In fact, we're so accustomed to this fast and frictionless way of shopping that the verb 'to Klarna' (meaning to make a BNPL purchase online) is a firm new fixture in our vocabulary. BNPL schemes risk putting many young people in Jess' position. Retailers offer credit for almost anything you want to buy on the internet, and it can all be arranged at the touch of a button. They are branded as 'no interest' (no APR), with Klarna's brand messaging suggesting that users 'hit snooze' if they need more time to make a payment, but if you miss your payment deadline after a further fifteen days your debt will be passed on to a debt collecting agency (Nelson, 2022). Missing payments on these schemes (or having several credit lines open at once, like Jess) can have a significant impact on your credit score and cost you your future financial freedom.

In contrast, Jess' best friend, Abigail, is the same age as her, had a similar job and roughly the same income. The only difference was that she focused on *keeping* some of her earnings by making regular savings each month for a deposit on her first home. Abigail still had fun. She went on nights out and she didn't live a frugal life by any means, but what she did do was make a habit of saving every month. She never got into credit card debt. She was able to buy her first flat at nineteen and stayed financially secure. She lived by the mantra of 'slow and steady wins the race'. Same income, similar lifestyles, and yet the financial decisions that they made led to one struggling with debt and one having her own flat. This was not an issue of inequality of income, but of *wealth inequality*.

Fortunately, once you're aware of the right way to manage your money, it's easy to reverse the situation. Since we started working together a few years ago, Jess has paid off all her credit card debt, used a Lifetime Individual Savings Accounts (LISA), and saved enough to buy her first house in just five years. Like Shaq, she also became aware of her habits and learned how to manage her money.

Note: There is, of course, a case for using credit and store cards. These can boost your credit score and support you at a time in your life when you might be applying for a mortgage. There are also people who feel more financially free with the safety net of a credit card for use in emergencies. If you can keep up to date with your payments, aren't at the top of your credit card limit every month, and don't have debt hanging around for lengthy periods of time, then credit cards can demonstrate that you are a responsible borrower.

The ravages of inflation

In the mid-1980s, my parents took a job in a school in Buenos Aires. Argentina at that time was suffering two of the nastiest concepts in money: inflation and devaluation. This meant that every month, the value of money was falling by a third – so 100 pesos on the first of the month was worth 70 pesos by the end of it. This presented my parents with several challenges. As a family, our earnings were effectively unstable. As Brits living in Argentina, it was risky to open a local bank account. My parents had to go to the bank to collect their salary in local currency – often a big wodge of notes. The same evening my dad and his friend would go to the house of the local black-market dealer (huge, gated and guarded by Dobermanns) to buy US dollars. It might sound shady having to change money on the black-market, but if they hadn't done that, their earnings would have soon been worthless.

Once home, my parents would put all the dollars in a hiding place in our house as they wanted to save up to buy a car and pay for our summer holiday. The next day, using our remaining local currency, we would go out to do our monthly grocery shop. It was like playing 'Supermarket Sweep', as often the price of food would change while we were shopping. My sister and I would race ahead of them to get the things we wanted at the lower price. Looking back, it was an incredible experience. Imagine if you got paid your monthly salary, and a month later, it was worth a third less. It might sound bizarre, and perhaps it was, but that's what it was like every month in Argentina. You could not afford to go to sleep on your money or you might wake up and find it gone. I remember losing my first tooth and getting a one million pesos note from the tooth fairy. Now that's inflation!

We learn our money saving habits by the age of seven, so my sister and I were acutely aware from a young age that when earning money, you might have to make some deliberate choices to *keep it* and *protect it* (Housel, 2020). To protect your earnings from the ravages of inflation, you need to keep and grow them to secure your future wealth and prosperity. You can do this by growing your money, which we'll discuss in Part Three.

In the UK, we have experienced a gentler rate of inflation of just over 2.6% a year for the last thirty years. This may not feel like much, but if inflation keeps rising, in ten years' time, your money will buy you around a third less than today. At the time of writing this, late 2022, inflation had risen to over 10% (ONS, 2022). If this continues, it means your money will halve in value. This should be less of a problem while you are working as hopefully your earnings can keep pace with inflation or you will earn more as you become more experienced and take on more responsibility. However, when you retire, you need to make the money you saved for retirement last for the rest of your life, which could be to a hundred years old. This means your retirement savings need to grow faster than inflation to ensure you can buy the same amount in years to come.

Streams of income

My parents earned average salaries. They were sensible, saved what they could and never got into debt. They were careful and kept their money (despite the hyperinflation in Argentina), grew their money when interest rates were high, and invested in property. They had mastered good habits around 'earning it, keeping it and growing it', so that, despite their circumstances, they were still able to give me pocket money in dollars. This was sensible – but meant I didn't have any pesos to spend on sweets in the school shop. So, how did I get my pesos? The school shop gave you money for returning empty drink bottles. Every day at school breaktime, I'd watch the older pupils drinking Coca-Cola and Fanta and leave their empty bottles lying in the playground. At the end of the day, I'd gather them up and return them to the shop to earn a few pesos. My entrepreneurial career had begun.

Nowadays, in the digital age, there are money-making opportunities everywhere. You can sell anything that you don't want on eBay, Gumtree or Facebook Marketplace. You can even make or sell your unwanted clothes on Depop. Monetising your hobbies has also become extremely popular, and some people are so successful that their 'side hustle' turns into their full-time job. When I founded a pensions consultancy business in 2006, I worked with a man called Tim Burton, who was part of the technology team. I still remember the day in May 2012 when he resigned to focus on his passion: supercars.

He had a YouTube channel, 'Shmee150', that was getting increasing views and subscribers. Google had spotted his trending channel showing videos of supercars in London and offered him a lucrative advertising opportunity for his channel. By 2022, he had amassed over 2.3 million subscribers on YouTube and 1.5 million followers on Instagram. His most popular video of a Lamborghini Aventador crash in 2014 has over 34 million views, and his channel has over a hundred videos with more than one million views (Anon, 2022). This makes him an undisputed car king of social media and one of the biggest supercar vloggers on the planet. Tim works super-hard: he is out filming every day, creating new compelling content for his viewers, and understands the importance of building a global brand that businesses want to partner with. He is truly living the dream and making money ('earn it') from what he loves most.

Income, not salary

When I was a teenager, my family eventually returned to England. My parents taught me how to drive but believed I should save up to buy my own car. I took a part-time job working as a hotel porter in Bristol. The car I bought was a Ford Fiesta, white with red stripes and a 957cc engine. It was no supercar, but for a seventeen-year-old, it was a nice car to drive, and to this day it is still my favourite car. I was able to buy that car because I had a plan. I knew exactly how many days I had to work to earn enough money to buy the car. What I hadn't anticipated was that my net wages ended up being a lot less than I was expecting because of taxation. I tweaked my plan and recalculated the number of extra days I needed to work. It was here that I learned that an *awareness* of your situation is essential to financial planning. Like Shaquille O'Neal, being aware of what tax I should have been paying on my earnings could have helped me plan better to achieve my goal.

Cars mean different things to different people. Shaquille O'Neal wanted the Mercedes because it was cool and coveted. My friend Tim is passionate about them, and they are his hobby. My first car got me from A to B, and I now drive an electric car, because it's important to me that I am environmentally responsible. What's key is to strike the right balance between what you need, what you like and what you can afford. It's popular to get cars on finance – which can work for some people but can also be a big financial commitment and affect your ability to save. We'll discuss budgeting in a later chapter, where we'll look at the importance of being in the driving seat when it comes to your finances.

***

The stories I've shared with you in this chapter demonstrate the importance of being able to *earn, keep and grow* your money. It is so important to build good habits and stay the course if you want to see the results. There are a few nuggets of financial wisdom that have become clichés for a reason, like 'paying yourself first' or 'saving for a rainy day'. Your financial resilience and freedom start by actioning some of those clichés and turning them into lifelong habits.

3

Understanding
Your Payslip

'What gets measured gets managed.'
— Attributed to Peter Drucker

Despite counting down the days until it lands in your account or celebrating with after-work drinks, the chances are that when your payslip finally arrives, you probably don't even open it, missing out on an opportunity to quite literally take your financial wellbeing into your own hands. Building a financially resilient life requires three key money moves: earning it, keeping it and growing it. Understanding your payslip is the first and most fundamental step to being able to keep and grow what you are already earning. (If you're yet to start work, or currently out of work, this chapter will be helpful for when you receive your first or next payslip.)

SALARY

− TAX + N.I.

_____

= WHAT YOU KEEP

It may sound simple (and even a little boring), but all good financial planning begins with being *aware* of your current situation. Shaq's million-dollar mistake was caused in part by him being unaware of his tax liability. With awareness and understanding, you can take appropriate actions – 'money moves' – to solve, rectify or boost your financial goals. Once you find your groove with these actions (your 'money mojo'), you can accelerate these steps to start making your money work for you. Whatever your current financial situation – whether you're struggling with debt, learning how to budget, considering investing, or have begun investing and want to diversify your portfolio – I want you to understand these three things:

1. Financial wellbeing isn't dependent on how much you earn.

2. Awareness will help you to take the right actions and accelerate your ambitions.

3. With the right knowledge, tools and a solid plan, you can overcome any financial challenges and start your journey to financial freedom.

Thanks to the many apps and gadgets available that track every element of our health, when it comes to our wellbeing, many of us are hyperaware of everything from the quality of our sleep and the number of calories we have consumed to our steps walked each day. When it comes to tracking our wealth, we're actually not very good at it. Around 85% of UK adults don't understand the tax or pension contributions on their payslips (Angeloni, 2021). We may be living in the age of Big Data, but the smaller numbers still count. Let's explore how you can improve your awareness of your earnings.

Understand the tax you're paying

Good mental wealth starts with a simple awareness of what you have now: your gross pay. Your gross pay is the amount you are paid before any deductions, so next time you look at your payslip, check that you are being paid the agreed amount. Gross pay includes overtime and bonuses, and these will usually be shown separately. If you're not sure how to calculate your gross pay, check your monthly payslip. Assuming there are no extras, you need to multiply the figure by twelve to check it matches your contracted annual salary.

Just like your Fitbit tells you how many daily steps you've racked up that day, it's worthwhile tracking how much tax you're paying. Your tax code on your payslip is assigned by the UK Tax Office (HMRC) and is made up of letters and numbers, reflecting how much of your earnings are tax-free. If you've paid too much tax, HMRC should contact you and pay you back through a tax code adjustment. In the situation where you've underpaid tax, you'll have to pay it back. Awareness of your financial situation should prevent the latter from happening – meaning you're not on the receiving end of a bill you weren't expecting to pay, which could impact your monthly budget or your long-term financial goals.

Salary 'deductions' don't necessarily mean going without

Next time you receive your payslip, look at your National Insurance (NI) contributions, which are deducted from your gross pay. You might consider your NI contribution a deduction from your hard-earned cash, but, as you'll come to see when I introduce you to your 'future self', you're not losing this money. You're simply moving it. You pay NI contributions towards your State Pension and the NHS. If you don't pay enough NI, you may jeopardise your rights to sick pay, jobseeker's allowance and a State Pension, so it's worth making sure the payments are correct.

Your state, employment and personal pension contributions will all appear on your payslip. Awareness of your pension contributions (or the steps you need to take to start contributing to your pension) all start by understanding what the numbers on your payslip really mean. You don't have to do this alone – the payroll team at your workplace will be able to walk you through each item on the list. You may also see deductions for your student loan, or benefits from your workplace like health or dental insurance. By looking at your payslip and making sure these are for the correct amount, you can stay on top of your net income each month, which will help you set, and stick to, a regular budget.

Now that you're aware of how to break down your payslip, where those deductions are going, and how they pay you back in time, in the next chapter I'm going to take you through the key principles of keeping it and growing it.

4

Become More Valuable: How To Increase Your Earning Potential

'Find a way to do more for others than anyone else does... And you will have the opportunity to earn more.'
— Tony Robbins

Regarding your journey to financial freedom, I've made the case that it's not how much you earn, but how much you keep and grow. While this is undoubtedly true, let's face it, building financial freedom is a lot easier when you're earning £60,000 a year rather than £30,000. This is because the more you earn, the more you can keep and the more you can grow.

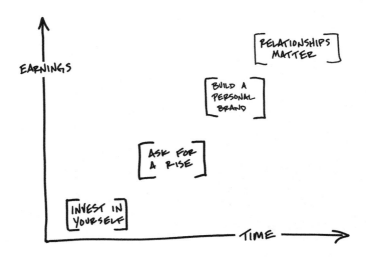

While money doesn't buy happiness, it can make life more comfortable, give you more options and greater peace of mind, and provide security for your future. Therefore, it's helpful to understand how you can become more valuable and increase your earning potential. In the next section are various strategies to help you do this.

Invest in yourself

We'll look at investment tactics to grow your money later, but it's worth remembering that you too are an asset, so one of the first steps you can take to increase your earning potential is to invest in yourself. Reid Hoffman, co-founder and CEO of LinkedIn, emphasises the importance of investing in yourself and continuously developing skills for your career in his book *The Start-Up of You* (Hoffman and Casnocha, 2013). Whether you choose to do this through further education, learning and development courses offered at work, or online courses and podcasts, investing in yourself helps you gain new skills, knowledge and experience that make you more valuable.

Analysis by the Institute of Fiscal Studies found that individuals with a university degree tend to earn around £3,000 more a year over the course of their career than those who do not (LBC 2020). But you haven't missed out if you don't have a university degree, because there are many educational opportunities available to help you further your career, including apprenticeships, vocational training and university courses.

In addition, your employer may offer various free or subsidised learning and development courses to support and grow you in your role. These will likely increase your earning potential because they make you more valuable to your company and eligible for a pay rise. The new skills and knowledge you gain can also be applied to other jobs in the future. Ideally, learn something that gives you a competitive advantage at the intersection of new skills and opportunities.

Learning a rare or highly paid skill is an excellent way to maximise your earning potential. This involves identifying the skills that are in high demand and developing expertise in those areas to make you more valuable, leading to higher salaries and more job opportunities. What if the relevant courses aren't readily available and accessible to you via your employer, though? In that case, you might need help finding where to seek free and credible courses likely to increase your value.

One example I recommend to people interested in technology roles is the Salesforce Trailhead programme. A former colleague of mine, Matthew, was looking to increase what he could offer as an employee and found Salesforce Trailhead a helpful way to reach his goal of securing a higher salary. Not only has he since learned new digital skills and earned recognised credentials, but he is also now part of Salesforce's community of 'trailblazers', who have access to over a million jobs to discover in the Salesforce ecosystem. The average salary for a Salesforce developer through Salesforce Trailhead is more than £100,000 per annum (more than three times the UK average salary). Matthew is now enjoying his new role earning over 50% more than before and on track to financial freedom.

Another way to grow your earnings is to seek opportunities in high-growth industries. A great place to learn which sectors are growing is LinkedIn's economic graph, which gives insights into over 60 million companies and 900 million members worldwide.

For example, the sustainability job sector is rich with opportunities, specifically in financial services, where jobs are well-paid. The Cambridge Institute for Sustainability Leadership offers several courses if you want to work in this area. You no longer need a traditional finance and economics degree to work in finance – asset and wealth managers are increasingly hiring people with marine biology and similar degrees to fill these new sustainability roles.

As well as courses and skills, remember to hold yourself accountable for continuously improving your job performance, like Basketball legend Michael Jordan who said, 'I've missed over 9,000 shots in my career. I've lost almost 300 games. 26 times I've been trusted to take the game-winning shot and missed. I've failed over and over and over again in my life. And that is why I succeed.' (Jordan, 1998). The more value you deliver for your team, boss and company, the more likely you will get raises, bonuses and promotions.

Consider getting a coach or a mentor to help you understand your story, strengths and passions, and unlock your value to make an even more significant impact. Michael Jordan had several coaches, including Phil Jackson, who helped him help the Chicago Bulls become one of the greatest teams ever. A coach or mentor can guide you to identify opportunities for career growth and increase your earnings.

Ask for a pay rise and a promotion

Asking for a pay rise can be daunting. In response to a survey of 3000 employees in the UK, more than half (55%) said they would not ask for a raise either because they wouldn't know what to say, are worried about looking greedy or are simply afraid (Kolb and Williams, 2021). Still, it's an essential step towards increasing your earnings, and can have substantial long-term benefits for your future self, as you will see later in this book. Finding the courage to have these conversations early in your career – for example, asking for a 10% increase in your starting salary – can lead to significantly higher earnings over a lifetime (Business Insider, 2017). This is definitely a conversation worth having, as Michael Jordan did with Nike in 1984, when he was a mere rookie and Nike was a fledgling brand. Instead of the usual royalty deal, Michael negotiated a percentage of future sales, and input on the design of the shoes and the new Air Jordan brand.

Wherever you are in your career and whatever you are working to negotiate, I suggest researching first and being prepared for the conversation, which will likely be worse in your head than in reality. Find the average salary for your job in your area and prepare a list of your achievements and contributions to your role, demonstrating that you are already acting competently above your salary bracket. Be confident and assertive, and don't be afraid to negotiate, because not only could this conversation grow your income, but it will also be a positive for your personal and professional growth – whatever the outcome.

Invest time in learning about negotiation by listening to podcasts, reading books and even signing up for a course. Then, get your coach or mentor to role-play asking for a pay rise. Take comfort that these conversations aren't only challenging to those just starting out in their careers, but whether they become easier over time depends on you and the circumstance. Often, the challenge is knowing your value and negotiating your worth, which can be demanding at every career stage.

For example, suppose you are currently applying for a senior promotion to managing director or partner. In this case, get an executive coach well in advance to help you prepare and maximise your potential.

Start a side hustle or set up your own business

As we learned from Tim, aka 'Shmee150', starting a side hustle or setting up a business can significantly increase your earning potential. Especially if it aligns with what you are good at and love. When it works, the pros are clear: it can provide you with an additional source of income and give you greater control over your financial future. However, starting a business can be challenging and risky, and it takes a lot of hard work and dedication to succeed.

If you're thinking of starting a business, it's essential to do your research and develop a solid business plan. Make sure you have a clear understanding of your target market, your competition and your costs. It's also essential to have a strong marketing plan in place to attract customers and promote your business. Again, do your research before you quit your job.

A great way to de-risk this strategy is to start your business as a side hustle while still working and earning a regular income, which is what Tim did. Starting a business doesn't even have to be about increasing your income. You can do it later in your career once you have honed your skills and discovered what drives you, what your values are and where you have built the necessary connections to give you the confidence to start.

For example, when publishing this book, I left my salaried role to change direction and start a new company. I co-founded Rebalance Earth, which is on a mission to create a world worth living in by reversing climate change and biodiversity loss, something I feel passionate about. While my new role excites me, it is a start-up with no regular salary to pay the monthly bills – so I have a side hustle as a non-executive director (NED) and business coach. In both roles, I am being paid for my advice, experience and knowledge in entrepreneurship, investing and sustainability, which I have built up over my career.

Go freelance

Going freelance is another option for increasing your earning potential. This involves working on a project-by-project basis, typically for multiple clients, rather than being employed full-time by one company. Free-lancing can be a great way to earn more for the same job as you have been doing as you can charge higher rates for your services. Additionally, freelancing allows you to have more control over your schedule and work remotely, which can save on travel costs.

For example, my friend Beth went freelance early in her career in public relations because she identified an opportunity to earn significantly more than she was, along with enjoying the freedom to work where and when she wanted. That suited her lifestyle. Over a decade into her career, she has increased her fees as time has gone on and her experience has grown, and is able to pick and choose the right jobs. As a result, Beth now has a portfolio of clients offering retained income to cover her regular bills and ad hoc projects giving her the freedom to travel for work.

Freelancing isn't for everyone. Those working for themselves are responsible for their own insurance, pensions (more on this later in the book) and taxes. Freelancers also have to manage unpredictable income, as work may only sometimes be available, so building your personal brand and reputation is essential.

Build your personal brand

Whether you're employed, freelance or an entrepreneur, protecting your reputation and standing out by positioning yourself as a thought leader and authority in your field is essential. If you do this well, you can attract more customers and opportunities if you are in business; and it raises your profile at the company you work for.

In 2012 when I was building my first business, Redington, I read a book, *Key Person of Influence* (KPI) by Dan Priestley. Then I went on to do his KPI course to help me build my personal brand and establish my credibility in the pensions industry. His insight was that you must invest in your personal brand. This is the perception people have of you, and it's crucial to create a strong and consistent brand that aligns with your values and goals.

I invested time in understanding what motivates me: financial education and sustainability. I then updated my social media profiles. Dan says if you don't exist on Google, you don't exist. He taught me to build a strong online presence by sharing my knowledge. I do this by regularly posting on Instagram, LinkedIn and Twitter on topics I am passionate about and have a unique perspective on. I also build my credibility by sharing my expertise and knowledge at conferences, writing articles, speaking on podcasts and being featured in the press. When I recently changed career to start my latest business, Rebalance Earth, I re-read Dan's book and signed up for his KPI course again to help me apply these skills in my new industry.

A former colleague and good friend, Anna, builds her personal brand well by highlighting topics that impact her clients. She does this by writing blogs and sharing her knowledge on LinkedIn. Her expert opinions mean she is regularly quoted and interviewed in the press, raising her profile across her industry.

She leads a team and has helped the team members increase their profiles by encouraging them to speak at conferences and write and share blogs on LinkedIn. This boosts each member's individual profile and that of the team as a whole, helping them all become more influential to their clients.

Relationships matter

In Reid Hoffman's podcast *The Start-up of You*, he shares a story about how George Clooney got his breakthrough acting job on *ER* (Hoffman, 2022). The main point Hoffman makes is that the best jobs and opportunities are attached to *people*. You need to know the right people, and they need to know, like and trust you. This means you must build and grow your network of relationships in advance.

A helpful framework comes from Andy Lopata, a professional relationships strategist. His insight is that professional relationships underpin business and career success (Lopata, 2020). Your contacts can provide advocacy, opportunities and support, yet not all people or businesses focus on building, nurturing or leveraging their relationships. Lopata's Seven Stages of Professional Relationships will help you understand where you are on this journey.

Stage one is, do people of influence recognise you? Two, do they know what you do? Three, do they like you? Four, do they trust you? This is key if you are going to work together. Five, do they support you? Six, are they an advocate? In other words, do they promote you and your work? Finally, stage seven is where you become good friends.

This framework has helped me enormously in understanding where I am in a relationship. For example, I know I am at level two or three if I meet someone at a conference and connect on LinkedIn. Getting to stage four, trust, requires investing time with them, ideally at least seven hours in more than one location. Yes, networking is essential, but the real work is in getting from stage three to four and beyond. Today, I still benefit from relationships I developed and nurtured over twenty years ago at the start of my career.

By applying the strategies we have covered here, you can increase your earning potential, but the key to building your financial freedom comes in three parts: how much you earn, how much you keep and how much you grow. By increasing your earning potential, you increase the money you keep and grow, significantly impacting your future wealth and progress to financial freedom. However, keeping hold of your money as your earnings increase and being disciplined about growing what you keep is more challenging than you might think.

PART TWO
KEEP IT

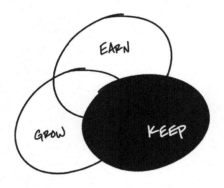

'Do not save what is left after spending; instead spend what is left after saving.'
— Warren Buffett

5

Building Your
Financial Resilience

'Beware of little expenses; a small leak will sink a
great ship.'
— Benjamin Franklin

Before we can enjoy financial freedom, we need to build financial resilience. When we think about our wellbeing, we generally consider our mental health. During the global pandemic, for example, mental wellbeing was front and centre for many people. How often do we ever think about our mental wealth? In this chapter, I'll show you how to achieve this and the steps you can take to prepare for unexpected financial setbacks.

There's a direct link between our wellbeing and our personal finance. Half of mental health issues come from owing money and being in debt, so learning how to build up your mental and money resilience is important (National Debt Line, 2020). Often, money worries are escalated by not knowing how to talk about our finances, or who to turn to, but we can all help reduce the stigma by having money conversations with the people we trust.

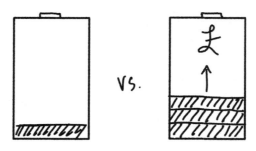

Personal resilience is about whether you have enough shock absorption in your system to prepare you for unexpected 'bumps in the road'. The same is true for your finances. You need a base layer of financial resilience in place that you will build on over the course of your lifetime, setting you up for these unexpected bumps and for when you finally stop work. This might include having enough savings in your bank account to cover things like a car repair, a lost phone or a broken boiler, while having enough left over to eat and pay your regular monthly expenses and your mortgage or rent. We need to be financially and mentally equipped to deal with these setbacks. Without financial resilience, we can fall into cycles of debt and can't plan for the future.

Imagine that your financial resilience is like the battery in your smartphone. Think about your current smartphone battery as though it was your money 'today'. If you're like me, you probably have battery anxiety: you wake up each morning, check your phone, and feel anxious if your battery is not fully charged, or if it drops below 20% while you're out and about without a charger. When your phone is fully charged, you're happy. This is how a lot of people feel about their money. When we get paid each month and see our bank balance rise, we feel happy. When it's low or we are in debt, we feel understandably anxious. When your phone is fully charged, you can do all the things you need to. You can listen to music, use all your apps, make phone calls, check your emails and so on. Over the course of the day, the battery will go down and, in the evening, you must charge it up again. The same is true with your bank account. You charge it by going to work and earning money, and when you buy things, it goes down. When your battery life is topped up, you can afford the essentials in life (food, transport, and a secure home) and the things you want to do, such as going to the gym, eating out and going on holiday.

Managing your smartphone battery is like budgeting your money – which many of us think we're dreadful at, because we've never learned or been taught how to do it. According to research published in *The Metro*, nine out of ten UK adults felt that they were not adequately taught life skills at school, with money management on top of the list (Scott, 2019). In fact, four of the top five life skills that UK adults wish that they had learned at school (as listed below) were related to money:

1. How to budget money

2. How to handle money

3. DIY skills

4. Mental health awareness

5. Taxes and living expenses

You can start managing your finances in the same way that you manage your phone battery. When your phone enters 'low power mode' or tells you that you've only got 20% battery left, you minimise your usage by turning off apps that are draining the battery. You stop listening to music, checking emails, or scrolling through social media to make sure that you're not going to completely run out of battery before you get home. Similarly, if you have an expensive month or need to use your emergency savings, what can you stop doing that will keep your finances in check? Be aware of your spending habits, and if you know you've had a lot of expenditure one month, take action to balance the scales by charging your wallet and saving some money. If you're not recharging your emergency savings, you could become financially vulnerable.

How can I build my cash buffer?

Life will, unfortunately, deliver setbacks to us all. The simple solution is to be prepared for the unexpected bumps in the road by creating a dedicated emergency fund. This is not a savings pot for long-term goals, but a 'level-up' on your battery life. As clichéd as it sounds, it's your 'rainy-day' fund. If the thought of creating this feels challenging, don't worry. You're not alone. Over half of UK adults do not have enough emergency savings (Hargreaves Lansdown, 2021). Getting into the habit of saving is simpler than you may think. It starts with becoming aware of your lifestyle and making a few adjustments each month. You can build up a cash buffer quickly, making sure you don't fall back into the red. The amount of emergency savings you need will depend on how old you are, whether you have dependants and where you are on your financial journey. It might be £100, £500, a month's rent, three months' expenses, or six months' wages.

Many people experience financial difficulty because their finances are permanently running on empty or 'low-battery mode'. Living month to month without a cash buffer means that when something unexpected happens, you don't have the money to fix it, and are forced to either go without or borrow money. Being in debt is the equivalent of being in constant low-battery mode, as Jane found out with her store cards. If you are in low-battery mode, your priority is to pay off your debt as soon as possible and charge up your 'today' fund. If you do this and are then able to create an emergency 'rainy-day fund' which you keep topped up, you will benefit from the peace of mind that comes from knowing you have savings to fall back on. Think of your rainy-day fund as the umbrella that will cover you today, weathering the storm, stress and worry that comes from being caught short on unexpected outgoings and preventing you from going into debt.

It's important to emphasise that people encounter financial difficulties for a whole range of reasons. As the cost of living continues to rise, more families across the UK will become financially vulnerable. If you're in serious debt or struggling to make ends meet, you're not alone. There are charities that can help you – a list is included at the end of this book.

Once you've got your emergency savings in place, how can you keep on top of your spending and saving each month? How we track and budget our money has changed a lot in the last twenty-five years. When I was at university, budgeting for a night out was simple. If I planned to spend £10 (worth over £20 at the time of publishing this book) that night, that is exactly what I would take with me in cash. Whether I spent the lot on drinks, saved some for cheesy chips on the way home, or came home with some change, I would know exactly how much my night out had cost me, based on what was or wasn't left in my wallet. There were no nasty surprises.

We now live in a world where everything is going digital. The rise of contactless payments means we are fast becoming cashless. In June 2022, the contactless limit for a single transaction had recently increased from £30 to £100. That's a substantial amount. It means any one of us can burn through £100 multiple times a day without having to withdraw, or even physically touch, the money we're spending. As you can imagine, this adds another challenge when it comes to the mindful spending required to keep ourselves out of 'low-battery mode' and saving for our future. Now, when you go on a night out, you can pay for just about anything on your smartphone – making it easy to spend a lot of money. When you're out socialising and close to maxing out your budget for the night, it's easy to dip into your banking app and move money over from your savings pot or account to buy another round without a second thought. Unfortunately, this increases the likelihood that you'll wake up the next day regretting how much you've spent (not to mention a likely hangover). If you can form the habit of keeping your money rather than spending it mindlessly, you'll be helping yourself build financial resilience.

It comes back to awareness. We all have good days with money and bad days with money. Do you know where or when you're most likely to spend impulsively? Maybe it's on a night out, or on clothes like Jane. It could be ordering takeaways, or trainers. Understanding what triggers your spending habits is one of the most powerful things you can do in taking action to improve your financial wellbeing. An important part of this is being aware of who, and what, you surround yourself with. Social media has become monetised, and influencers like to sell us things and promote a lifestyle of material goods or big nights out in abundance. Do the people in your life or the accounts you follow promote healthy money habits? Are there accounts you could follow to help balance out your feed?

Creating a 'tomorrow' fund

Now, here's the magic part. If you're *earning* your money and you're *keeping* hold of your money because you're managing your today fund, you can start thinking about *growing* your money to achieve your goals. For many young adults, a key financial priority is saving to buy a home. Creating a 'tomorrow fund' is a great way to do that. This is exactly what Jane did once she had paid off her store card debt: she topped up her today fund and started saving into her tomorrow fund for a deposit on her first home. Your tomorrow fund is also a great way to plan and fund those lifechanging bucket list things you want to do, like taking a year off to travel around the world. One of my friends wants to dive the Titanic. It costs about £100,000, and her tomorrow fund is helping her save to achieve this.

Savings for your retirement will go into your 'day-after-tomorrow fund'. The cool thing is that once you start saving money into your day-after-tomorrow fund, you start to benefit from the magic of compound growth. Many of us will do this at work via our work-place pension, but there are often opportunities and 'free' money to encourage us to save even more. If you are self-employed and don't have a pension, I recommend setting up your own day-after-tomorrow pension fund and paying into it every month.

Let's recap on the three funds you can top up to build financial resilience and freedom:

1. Your 'today fund' needs to be kept in cash. It's there to smooth out the bumps in the road. It builds financial resilience and will protect you from going into debt and/or having to stop saving for your future.

2. Your 'tomorrow fund' is for long-term goals and aspirations like buying your first home, getting married and ticking off your bucket list.

3. Your day-after-tomorrow fund is for your retirement and future prosperity. The riskiest

thing that you can do with this fund is to keep it in cash. This fund needs to be invested in a diverse portfolio of global shares, bonds and properties to beat inflation and grow to fund your retirement. I'll explain how you can do this later in the book.

Now you know how, the hard bit is making this into a habit of a lifetime. The key is awareness of your spending and saving habits, and an action plan for how you can make small changes that will shore up your ability to deal with setbacks and save for the long term. As James Clear says, 'Habits are the compound interest of self-improvement' (Clear, 2021). If, like me, you are not good at sticking to your habits, the best way to 'keep it' is to set up an automatic direct debit to your savings on the day you get paid. You can choose to automate this into both your today fund and your tomorrow fund. If you set up a direct debit, even if it's only for a small amount each month, you'll make sure that your rainy-day fund is always fully charged. You'll quickly learn to live on what's left, and that's the best way to achieve long-term financial freedom. Many digital banking apps allow you to have saving 'pots' within your current account, which has made keeping it easier than ever. To double up on your good habits, you'll also want to put money away in your day-after-tomorrow fund. Again, the easiest way to do that is via a direct debit going out at the beginning of each month.

6

Weatherproofing Your Finances

'Pay yourself first.'
— **George Clason, *The Richest Man in Babylon***

Now you understand how to build your rainy-day fund and top it up when necessary, I'm going to share some stories which show how having a rainy-day fund will help you weather financial storms on your path to financial freedom.

I love the Bible story and musical about Joseph (and his amazing technicolour dream coat). It's about being aware that the future is uncertain and finding a way to take action to smooth out those 'bumps in the road'. Joseph was beaten up and sold into slavery by his jealous brothers. He eventually ends up in jail in Egypt, where he discovers that he has a gift for interpreting dreams. He goes on to interpret the dreams of Pharaoh, who tells Joseph,

> 'I dreamed that I was standing on the bank of
> the Nile, when seven cows, fat and sleek, came
> up out of the river and began feeding on the
> grass. Then seven other cows came up which
> were thin and bony. . . The thin cows ate the
> full ones.' (Book of Genesis)

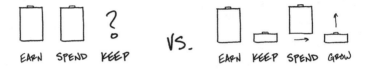

Joseph tells Pharaoh that the dreams mean there are going to be seven years of plenty, but these will be followed by seven years of famine, which will ruin the country. When Pharaoh asks Joseph what he can do about it, Joseph replies,

> 'Take a fifth of the crops during the seven
> years of plenty. . . The food will be a reserve
> supply for the country during the seven years
> of famine which are going to come on Egypt.
> In this way the people will not starve.' (Book
> of Genesis)

Pharaoh does what Joseph suggests and puts aside a fifth (the golden rule of saving 20% of what you earn) of all the food that is harvested during the time of plenty. The result is that no one starves during the famine and Pharaoh appoints Joseph to govern over all Egypt.

Be like Pharaoh

The reason I like this story is because it teaches us that the future is uncertain, the one thing that we can be sure of is that there will be both good and bad times, and history has a habit of repeating itself.

I like to go hill walking. A few years ago, I climbed Ben Vrackie, a mountain in Scotland, with a friend. In the carpark at the bottom of the mountain, there's a sign asking, 'Are you prepared?' It always amazes me how many people I see get out of their cars in shorts, t-shirts and trainers and set off to walk to the top of the mountain without a care in the world. The sign also warns that the weather may change quickly and without warning, and that you need to be prepared for whatever the weather might throw at you. 'Plan your journey, take warm and waterproof clothing. Food and drink. Wear sound boots and carry a map and compass.' Sadly, despite the signs, every year people get stuck on mountains like Ben Vrackie and end up in serious trouble because they are simply not prepared for the changing weather and its impact. The sign doesn't stop us from enjoying the wonderful walk to the summit of Ben Vrackie. Whatever the season, we can always go up the mountain, but we need to be prepared for the climb and the unpredictability of the weather.

The same applies to your money journey and building a happy and prosperous financial future. The key to building financial resilience is being aware that the one thing we can be certain of is uncertainty, and to prepare for the bad times, or the unexpected, by putting aside 20% of the harvest during the good times. We can have a financial plan in place but need to be agile when things happen that we couldn't see coming, for example, suddenly being made redundant. This is like the weather changing when you're halfway up Ben Vrackie. If you've got nothing in your rucksack, what are you going to do? If you've got no financial reserves in your today fund, then losing your job could be disastrous for you and your family. We talked about the stress and anxiety caused by money difficulties, especially from owing money and being in debt. Before you start to think about growing your money, it's important to build financial resilience. Once you have mastered this, you can focus on building long-term prosperity and financial wellbeing.

What if you haven't built up those reserves to have financial resilience? What do you do when you lose your job, or your business revenues collapse overnight? Just like hiking on Ben Vrackie, where the weather can change quickly or without warning, you must make tough decisions. This happened to my friend, Paul. His story shows the unpredictability of life and the importance of being financially aware, taking action when and where you need to, and accelerating or changing plans at short notice.

Paul is an old friend who now lives in Mexico with his wife and children. He founded a business running schools that teach English as a foreign language. Over the years, he's been successful, and he earns a good living to support his family. Unfortunately, Mexico was particularly badly hit by the global pandemic. Paul was forced to shut down all his schools with no notice. Overnight, he went from having a good income to having no income at all. Paul was terrified. He'd hit a real crisis point. He had a house, his children were in a private school, they went on family holidays, and suddenly he'd run into financial difficulty overnight – with no warning. This happened to many business owners and entrepreneurs around the world as countries went into lockdown.

What Paul did as soon as the pandemic hit was to quickly go into 'low power' mode. He realised that to save his business, he had to pivot and go digital, which involved shifting to teaching his students online. His revenues were lower, but his overheads were, too. He still had a lot of expenses and needed to radically reduce his outgoings if he was going to survive without burning through all his reserves, so he took drastic action. He sold his house and rented a smaller one to free up capital. He pulled his children out of private school and sold his car. In just a few weeks, he'd cut his expenditure by a massive two-thirds. By doing so, Paul was able to rebuild his financial resilience. He topped up his financial battery, which allowed his business to get back on track, kept his family fed and a roof over their heads. Their life was not as comfortable as it had been, but it wasn't long before Paul was able to pivot and rebuild his business so they could start enjoying their old lifestyle again. The point is that if he had not switched to low power mode when he did, he could well have lost everything.

Paul's story is a brilliant example of financially resilient behaviour and responding to uncertainty with awareness and action. His course of action sounds extreme, and it was. Most people will not have to sell their house to make themselves financially resilient – it's more likely to involve reducing their monthly outgoings by not going out as much, and perhaps changing their cars or halting home improvements. When things go wrong, you may need to move quickly. If you're walking up Ben Vrackie and the weather changes, then you don't carry on walking in your shorts and a t-shirt. You stop, you put on your fleece and your waterproofs, and you stay dry. You might even seek shelter for the weather to blow over. By not agonising over his decision, Paul was able to save himself, his family and his business. If you hit a financial crisis point in your life, waiting for a couple of months to see if it stops raining risks adding to the problem. The truth is, a sudden change in circumstances (or a global situation that we could never have predicted, like the pandemic) can put any one of us just two or three steps away from financial vulnerability. Part of our journey to build up long-term financial resilience is to keep in mind that the unexpected should be expected, and to weatherproof the money we have worked to earn and keep sheltering us from the storms.

Find a recent bank statement and make a note of all the things that you could cut out. What are the luxuries that you could do without? Where might you save money? Cancel all the direct debits that aren't vital. Have a think about whether you really need that subscription. What else could you do with that money? This exercise will save you money that will accumulate over the course of the year. By saving this money instead of spending it, you will start to charge your 'today' battery, which builds your financial resilience.

Most people are not wired to save, and many people regularly find that they don't have any money left over at the end of the month. This means that they are not financially resilient in the short term, and so are unable to build their financial reserves in the long term. By having more conversations about money and being aware of our habits and our goals, over time we can feel more confident about saving and more protected by the habits we have put in place. When we have become financially resilient, we can then think about *growing* our money.

7

Tax Wrappers Matter

'In this world, nothing is certain except death
and taxes.'
— Benjamin Franklin

Before we move on to growing your money,
I want to explain the different types of tax wrappers available to encourage you to save, invest and
help grow your money faster. The government has
created several different tax wrappers to help us invest for the long term, and many of us aren't aware
of them.

Normally when you invest, the growth on your
investment is either in the form of interest or dividends (which you'd normally pay income tax on), or
the growth from your investments (which you pay

capital gains tax on). When you invest using a tax wrapper such as an ISA or pension, these are tax-free.

$$\frac{\text{Grow your money} - \text{Tax}}{} = \text{What you keep}$$

Wrappers offer several different methods of investing your money in a tax-efficient way, and if you're not familiar with them you can end up missing out. Commonly used wrappers are ISAs, LISAs, JISAs and pension plans. There are others that are available depending on your personal circumstances and your tax position, but the ones I've mentioned are the main ones.

Different wrappers have different tax exemptions. For example, an ISA is Tax, Exempt, Exempt (TEE), which means the money you invest has already been taxed (T), the growth on investments is tax-free (E), and when you take your money out to use it, it's also tax-free (E).

A pension is the other way round: Exempt, Exempt, Tax (EET), which means that when you put money in a pension, you get free money from the government depending on how much tax you pay (E). Your capital growth is tax-free (E), but when you retire and start taking the money out, only 25% is tax-free. The rest you pay tax on (T). I'll explain how you can benefit from all of this in a later chapter.

Remember, when you earn money, you pay tax, which is why it's important that you understand your payslip. The more you earn, the more tax you pay. At the time of writing in late 2022, if you earn between £50,000 and £150,000, you pay 40% tax. Any money you earn above £150,000 is taxed at 45%.

But beware of the '60% tax trap'. If you earn between £100,000 and £125,000, you will effectively experience a 60% tax rate. This is because for every £2 you earn over £100,000 each year, you lose £1 worth of your tax-free personal allowance. One of the main things you can do to avoid the trap is to increase your pension contributions. By making pension contributions on any excess income you earn over £100,000, you can effectively prevent your taxable income from going into the 60% tax trap. I recommend getting professional advice to understand how to maximise your annual pension allowances.

A LISA is Exempt, Exempt, Exempt (EEE), which means the government gives you free money to invest: £1 for every £4 (E). The growth on your money is tax-free (E) and when you take the money out to buy a house, in retirement (at sixty years old) or if diagnosed with a terminal illness, this money remains tax-free (E).

FR££DOM: EARN IT KEEP IT GROW IT

Tax relief on	ISA	LISA	Pension
Annual Allowance	£20,000	£4,000	£40,000
Income	No	£1 for every £4	20% / 40% / 45%
Growth	Yes	Yes	Yes
Withdrawal	Yes	Yes	25%
Inheritance	No	No	Yes

Many wrappers such as ISAs and pensions have a limit as to what you can pay in. Making best use of your tax allowances means you can potentially save more for your future without significantly reducing your net income, and when you do grow your money, you maximise the amount you keep by not having to pay tax on your dividends or capital gains on your growth. And just to make it clear, you don't have to have a huge amount of money, or live in a certain postcode, to be able to access these government incentives. These wrappers are *open to everyone,* and if you don't have money to invest now, parents or grandparents can also contribute to help maximise your savings or support you getting on the property ladder. Even children (including babies) who aren't earning money have allowances and can still open a pension and benefit from tax wrappers. In fact, later in the text I'll show you how you can make your child a millionaire in retirement for just £5 per day.

Individual Savings Accounts (ISAs)

The simplest way to invest while taking advantage of tax relief is in an ISA. The money that you take out at the end is tax-exempt, so if you invest £10,000 and it grows to be £30,000 over the course of your investment, you don't pay any tax on that growth. Usually, if you invest £10,000 in shares and those shares go up in value from £10,000 to £30,000, you'd have to pay what's called capital gains tax on the money you earned. With ISAs, the government has created a framework that incentivises people to save for the long term by reducing the amount of tax that people pay on the growth. It used to be the case that you could only invest up to £7,000 a year in an ISA, but that limit has now been increased to £20,000 a year.

There are two types of ISA that you can invest in: a cash ISA, or a Stocks and Shares ISA. For the best long-term return on your investments, you'll want to invest in a Stocks and Shares ISA. When interest rates are low (below inflation), the amount of tax that you're going to save by having your money in a cash ISA is extremely low, so it may be better to switch the cash in your tomorrow fund into stocks and shares. It's easy to do, and if you have a cash ISA already, you can make the switch online in a couple of minutes.

Junior Investment Savings Accounts (JISAs)

These work in the same way as LISAs but can be opened for children under the age of eighteen. JISAs are a great way to help children save up for university fees, to go travelling or for a deposit on a house. If you open an account for your child when he or she is a baby, you can ask friends and relatives to contribute at Christmas and birthdays instead of spending money on gifts which may not last and don't support their future financial freedom or the future of the planet. If you start saving when the child is young, even if you're only saving tiny amounts each month, you're taking advantage of the stock market, the tax relief and compound interest to grow that money in the fastest way.

It is important to remember that when the child turns 18, they have full access and entitlement to the money. The money they have received in gifts is now irrevocably theirs, so fostering good money habits is essential. I cover this in the last chapter on how to leave a financial legacy.

Lifetime Savings Accounts (LISAs)

LISAs are a category of ISA which is designed to encourage people between the ages of eighteen and forty to save to buy a home. If you invest your money in a LISA, the government will give you 25p for every pound that you invest, for free. For example, if you invest £1,000 in a LISA, the government will give you £250. If you don't want to use the money that you've saved in your LISA to buy a house, you can keep saving your money in there until you are fifty years old, and then you can access that money, tax-free, when you're sixty and spend it on anything you want. You can't take the money out before you're sixty without incurring penalties, unless you're using it to buy your first home or you're diagnosed with a terminal illness.

LISA regulations (gov.uk)

- You can put in up to £4,000 each year, until you're fifty. The government will add a 25% bonus to your savings, up to a maximum of £1,000 per year.

- The LISA limit of £4,000 counts towards your annual ISA limit. This is £20,000 for the 2020 to 2021 tax year.

- You can hold cash or stocks and shares in your LISA or have a combination of both.

- When you turn fifty, you will not be able to pay into your LISA or earn the 25% bonus. Your account will stay open, and your savings will still earn interest or investment returns.

- To open and continue to pay into a LISA, you must be a resident in the UK, unless you're a crown servant (for example, in the diplomatic service), their spouse or civil partner.

How to use a LISA to get on the property ladder

One of the biggest issues facing young people is not being able to buy their own home. Many young people believe that they can't afford to buy a home, but using a LISA makes it more achievable. I'm going to show you how, with the help of a quick exercise, you can use one to help you get the deposit for a home in ten years.

The average cost of a house deposit in the UK (excluding Greater London) is somewhere between £25,000 and £40,000. Greater London is the most expensive region for first-time buyers, with an average deposit of over £100,000 (Statista, 2022).

This is a lot of money, so it's not surprising that many young people think it's out of their reach, but by using the 'earn it, keep it, grow it' approach to managing your money, you can save and invest enough to buy a new home in ten years. Use a notebook to calculate the figures below (I've used myself as an example):

1. **What's your daily (or weekly) vice?** Mine is a coffee at the train station and a sandwich lunch, which I buy every day at work. (For you, it could be Friday night drinks after work, a Netflix subscription, Amazon Prime or getting your nails done every month.) Calculate how much you spend per day on this vice. I spend about £10 a day on coffee and lunch.

2. **What is the annual price of that vice?** Now calculate how much you spend on your daily vice in a year. If I'm spending £10 a day at work, that adds up to £50 a week (five working days), which is about £2,500 a year (assuming 50 weeks).

3. **Are you willing to sacrifice your vice for a decade?** Now that you know how much your vice costs you yearly, what are you spending over a decade? Mine multiplied by ten gives me £25,000 that I could have saved.

4. **What if you saved your vice in a LISA?** Now multiply that figure by 1.25 (I'll explain why below). Mine gives me £31,250 (1.25 x £25,000).

5. **Invest, and your vice is thrice as nice:** Finally, multiply that figure by 1.5 (I'll explain why below). My result is £46,875 (1.5 x £31,250). That's enough for a deposit anywhere outside Greater London.

What number have you come up with? Are you surprised? How does it make you feel? The figure on your piece of paper is the amount of money that you could keep and grow over ten years towards buying a house. Now I'm going to explain to you how you got to it. I asked you to multiply how much you saved over ten years by 1.25. This is because the government wants you to save, and gives you 25p for every pound that you invest in a LISA. So, if you were to save £1,000, you get a £250 top up for free. (And who doesn't love free money?)

I then asked you to multiply that figure by 1.5. This is the amount of compound growth you may receive on your money if you invest and grow your savings over ten years by investing in a Stocks and Shares LISA. This will feel risky, as markets go up and down. Note: By automating your savings on a regular basis (for example, monthly), it helps to smooth out the ups and downs.

Assuming you can earn an average rate of 7% growth over ten years from being invested in a diversified mix of equities, bonds and properties, the 'Rule of 72' (discussed in a later chapter) means that you can double your money every ten years. The money you invested in year one doubles while the money you invested in year ten only grows 7%, so, on average, money saved on a regular basis over ten years grows about 1.5 times.

The reality is that there are people in the UK who genuinely don't have enough money, but for many, it's more achievable than they may think or know. Hopefully this quick exercise has shown you that it is possible for someone on an average salary to save enough money in ten years for a deposit on a house, or certainly a healthy start towards one. You just have to exchange one of today's vices for prosperity in the future. If you are thinking about saving for a home, then understand that the coffee, the one you buy on the way to work every morning, isn't *just* costing you £2.50 – it's costing you nearly £4.70 against your future house deposit. That way, you can make a better choice about what's important to you.

Why don't you have a go? Start by looking at your bank account. Go through all your direct debits and standing orders. You'll have subscriptions; what can you trim back on and turn into a deposit in ten years' time? What are you prepared to give up buying to buy your future house? You might not be planning to buy a house right now, but at least you know how to create a plan to buy a house if you do. In 2020, during the pandemic we saw a sharp drop in spending and an increase in saving. Jess did just that and has gone from store card debt to having bought her first home in five years – a great example of ordinary things, consistently done, to produce extraordinary results.

We'll talk about being wealthy versus being rich and understanding your net worth in a later chapter. Owning your own home is an important part of growing your overall wealth. A key reason why there's so much wealth inequality in the UK is because most people don't understand tax relief, so don't take advantage of the *free money* that the government will give you if you invest your money in a couple of specific ways. For most people, setting up an ISA and sorting out their pension will make a huge difference to their financial freedom. Once you've formed the good money habits that set you up on your path to financial freedom, you can help future generations by considering pensions and JISAs for your children and grandchildren; helping to break the cycle of debt and financial illiteracy that many of us have found ourselves stuck in.

Pension plans

Essentially, the government wants to incentivise you to save for your pension. One of the ways they do this is by allowing you to save into a pension from your gross income rather than from your net income, which means that you don't pay tax on the money that you contribute from your salary to your pension. During the time that your money is invested in your pension scheme, any growth that is earned is tax-free. Many larger companies will also have a contribution matching scheme, which you could take advantage of.

When you take money out of your pension, you *do* pay tax. This may sound boring or even a little confusing, but if you want to make sure your 'future self' is well looked after, I can't stress how important it is to understand this. If you don't have the time or the energy to get to grips with it yourself, then go and find someone who can help you make the most of your money. I promise it will be worth it, both for your peace of mind and for your future financial freedom.

What if you're a high earner?

If you're a high earner, and let's define that as someone who earns over £150,000 a year, then the amount that you can put into your pension gets capped by what's called the 'annual allowance'. It basically means that once you've invested the maximum, you may feel less inclined to invest further because there is no additional tax benefit. One thing you can do with your money once you've invested the maximum into your pension is to invest in riskier investments with higher returns.

One of the things that the government is trying to do is encourage people to invest in riskier start-up investments in an effort to support entrepreneurism and grow the economy. There are schemes like the Venture Capital Trust (VCT), the Enterprise Investment Scheme (EIS) and the Seed Enterprise Investment Scheme (SEIS), which are designed to give large tax breaks to high-income earners in return for investing their money in riskier start-up businesses. It's important to note that these funds are for people who have already taken care of themselves and their children and who are financially secure, or wealthy. These investment opportunities offer high returns, but they are also high-risk, and any money invested could be lost. If you can afford to lose your money, then go ahead and invest in these types of funds. If you can't afford to lose the money, then please steer clear of them. I have invested in these types of funds, but the money that I invest is not the money that is going to put my children through school or pay for my retirement. As long as you're prepared to lose all of your invested money and you look after yourself and your family first, then VCT, EIS and SEIS can be an interesting way to grow your funds, but don't do that exclusively. And don't do it until you've taken care of everything else first.

Why inheritance tax matters

Many people don't realise just how much tax needs to be paid at the time of their death, and often end up paying more to the taxman (HMRC) than they realise. It's a common misconception that when you die, you'll just leave your house to your dependants and that will be enough to sort them out financially. That's just not the case, because the first thing that happens when you die is that any surviving relatives could be hit with an inheritance tax bill. Even worse news is that they'll have to pay any tax bill within six months. This means that they'll either have to sell the family home as quickly as possible (and potentially at a lower price than it's worth) or have to find a way of paying the tax bill by the six-month deadline, because after this date HMRC will add interest.

You might not feel particularly wealthy, but trust me, when the taxman comes calling, he's going to be looking at everything, which is why it's useful to understand your net worth. He's going to look at all your assets, your property, your bank account, your shares, your investments, your jewellery, the contents of your house and your art – basically everything that you own. From that total sum (which can be much more than you think), he will subtract your inheritance tax allowance (you need to look this up at www. gov.uk/inheritance-tax) and then your dependants will have to pay 40% tax on anything that's left over. Only after the taxman has had his cut will the rest get split up according to your will.

In many cases, your family may end up with a lot less than you want them to have, and a lot less than they were expecting. This means that not only do you leave them with the emotional trauma, but they'll also have to sort out your financial affairs and could lose out on a lot of the money that they were counting on for their inheritance. The good news is that with careful financial planning, you can reduce your inheritance tax. There are ways to minimise what you pay, for example, by gifting money before you die, donating to charity and setting up trust funds. The HMRC website (www.gov.uk/government/organisations/hm-revenue-customs) is a useful resource for understanding how inheritance tax – the rules, allowances and thresholds – work.

PART THREE

GROW IT

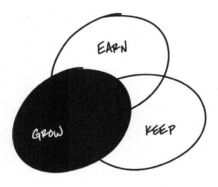

'The best time to grow your money was twenty years ago. The second-best time is now.'
— Based on an old Chinese proverb

8

Meet Your Future Self

'The highest form of wealth is the ability to wake up every morning and say, "I can do whatever I want today." The ability to do what you want, when you want, with who you want, for as long as you want, is priceless.'
— Morgan Housel

W hen growing your wealth, it's essential to include not only your tomorrow fund, but also your day-after-tomorrow fund, or your pension. Getting an early start on planning for your retirement doesn't mean going without now. In fact, it is a key part of financial wellbeing. The future often seems a long way off. It can be quite difficult to plan for the long term when you really have no idea what the world will look like thirty years from now. The thing to remember is that you're not saving for something abstract – what you're saving for is you. You are putting money away for your future self.

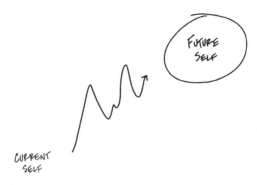

Because we don't know our future selves, we find the idea of creating a comfortable life that we will enjoy later down the line hard to imagine and act upon. One of the things I find helpful is to visualise my future self by using an ageing app. Looking at a picture of me in my seventies really helps me connect the financial decisions I'm making now with my future. I then find it easier to align my plan with my goals to make 'future Rob' happy and to give him a comfortable life that's free from financial worry. This is true financial wellbeing. Why don't you try it yourself? What can you do now to make sure that your future self has a nice life? Take a couple of minutes to sit down and really think about your answers to the questions below. These will be your first steps towards connecting with, and meeting, your future self:

- At what age do you want to retire?
- Have you thought about how long you might live?
- Do you know how much you'll need to retire on?
- Have you got a plan for how you're going to save up the money you will need in your retirement?
- Do you have a company or personal pension?
- Do you know how much you're saving in it?
- Do you know how much it's currently worth?
- Do you know how much it'll be worth when you retire?
- Does your company match your pension contributions?
- Do you have more than one pension?

If you don't know the answers to these questions, make it a priority to find out. Your payroll department will be able to help you and you can also seek advice from the Money & Pensions Service (https://maps.org.uk) or a financial advisor. Keep a record of your answers – it will be useful to revisit them every so often to make sure you're on track to retire when you want to and achieve your financial goals.

During the global pandemic in 2020, inspirational pensioner Captain Tom Moore raised over £30 million for the NHS by completing 100 laps of his garden before his hundredth birthday. The interesting thing about Captain Tom is that, when he retired in 1985, he probably didn't expect to live to be 100. When he retired, the average life expectancy for a man was about 76, and he probably needed about £10,000 a year to live comfortably. If he expected to live to 76, he would have needed about £110,000, right? Not quite. Because of inflation (the rise in the costs of goods and services over time), by the time he reached 99, he would have needed £30,000 a year to meet the same standard of living (PLSA, 2022).

What his story shows us is that we don't know how long we'll live, but we do know that the cost of living rises over time. We need to save more than we think we do for retirement. Investing the money you save into your day-after-tomorrow fund is how you can secure your financial future, because this is the best way to outpace inflation, so your money has grown in value by the time you come to retire.

How do I invest into my pension?

Pay As You Earn (PAYE)

If you're employed, your employer must, by law, offer you a pension. If you're on PAYE, the simplest way to invest for the future is to make sure you take advantage of your company's pension scheme. It's simple. Chances are you have already been automatically enrolled but take the time to find out if your company offers a matching scheme. If they do, make sure you take full advantage of it. If you don't, you're potentially turning down a free pay-rise to your future self.

Self-invested Personal Pension (SIPP)

If you're self-employed, you can get a pension with a private pension provider. If you're not sure which provider to get a pension with, you can visit the Money Advice Service website (www.moneyadvice-eservice.org.uk) and they will be able to point you in the right direction. It's also worth knowing that having a pension through your employment doesn't mean that you can't also invest in a private pension if you'd like to. Some people have two or even three different pensions that they invest into, so they can access different pots of money at different times once they've retired. You can also make Additional Voluntary Contributions (AVCs) to some employee pension schemes if you want and are able to.

People often think that by saving into a pension, they're losing money. Rest assured you are not losing money. What you're doing is moving money away from your today fund into your day-after-tomorrow fund. Think of it as gifting today's money to your future self. And remember, the sooner you start, the more time it has to grow, and the more your future self will thank you. The great thing about doing this is that when you save money into a pension, your employer and the government will also give you extra money for your future self.

The age-old question

'How much money do I need to retire?' is perhaps the most important question you should be asking yourself about your finances. One in three Brits don't know how big a pension pot they'll need, and one in five don't know how much they have (Green, 2020).

I'm asked this question a lot. I always advise gaining clarity on how and when you want to retire, so you can work backwards to calculate how much to save. A good rule of thumb is to have a pot worth ten times your annual salary by the time you retire. This sounds like a lot, but it's achievable by starting early and breaking it down into simple steps – like setting a savings goal for every decade you're in employment. Despite being a pensions expert, when I co-founded Redington (a pension consultancy), I didn't have one myself. I'd made the mistake that so many of us make – I was time-poor and the last thing I wanted to do at the end of a long day or at the weekend was to plan for my retirement. At the time I was young, and 'future Rob' wasn't a priority.

The pension that your future self will receive comes from three sources: the government (your State

Pension), your employer's contributions (deducted from your PAYE salary) and any personal contributions you want to add on top of that.

The State Pension is currently £185 per week (Gov.uk, July 2022). For most of us, this won't be enough to live off entirely. If you want to make sure you have a pot of money that lasts the rest of your life, factors in inflation and perhaps even a legacy for your loved ones, you will need to consider personal contributions to your pension. For future generations, the State Pension may look different – or not even exist. That's why it's so important for those of us reading this book to impart financial knowledge and literacy to our friends, children and grandchildren. It's only going to become more important as governments have to adapt to populations getting older. The only certainty is uncertainty, which is why we need to be like Pharoah and set aside a fifth of what we have during the 'years of plenty' (ie, when we are working), so that we have financial freedom when we retire.

When saving for a long-term goal like retirement, it's helpful to work backwards from the desired result to give you an idea as to what your retirement could look like. Here are three different budgets to consider for your future self. Remember that although pensions (EET) are tax-exempt on the way in, you will need to pay tax on the way out:

- **Minimum: £11,000 a year for a single person, or £17,000 for couples.** You can meet all your needs, plus enough for some fun. For example, you could holiday in the UK, eat out about once a month, and do some affordable leisure activities about twice a week. The good news is that through a combination of the full State Pension of £185 per week, and auto-enrolling in your workplace pension, this should be achievable for most people.

- **Moderate: £21,000 a year for a single person, or £31,000 for couples.** You can achieve financial security and more flexibility. For example, you could have a two-week holiday in Europe and eat out a few times a month, and the opportunity to do more of the things you want to do.

- **Comfortable: £34,000 a year for singles, or £50,000 for couples.** You can enjoy some luxuries like regular theatre trips, dining out and three weeks' holiday in Europe a year.

These examples assume that most people do not have a mortgage, rent or social care costs when they reach retirement. It's also worth bearing in mind that some people choose to pay off their mortgage when they retire and so might not have as much income as they think they will.

The average amount that you need to be saving into a pension is at least 15% of your annual salary. In the UK, if you are employed, the minimum your employer can save is 8% (3% from the employer and 5% from you), which is what most people do.

Note that this 8% is on qualified earnings between a lower earnings limit of £6,240 and an upper earnings limit of £50,270. Again, I have met people who get caught out by this. For example, if they are earning £100,000 and putting 8% into their pension, they think they are saving £8,000. Still their employer was only paying in 8% of qualifying earnings, which meant they were saving £3,522.40 (8% of £50,270 - £6,240). Again, it's worth checking with your employer or seeking financial advice.

This is a lot less than the recommended 15% needed to achieve a 'moderate' retirement. You need to save closer to 20% to achieve a 'comfortable' income in retirement, so if you're earning £35,000 a year, you need to be saving £7,000 a year into your pension.

The good news is, for many people, this doesn't mean you personally need to be saving £7,000 a year. Your employer probably pays into your pension. Your employer may also match additional contributions that you make to top up your pensions, which the government also gives you tax relief on. So, how much do you personally need to put in to hit that goal of 20% of your salary? You may be surprised to know it's less than £120 per month. Here's how:

- John is thirty years old and earning a salary of £35,000 a year.

- His company pays 10% of his salary a year into his pension. That's £3,500 a year (or £291.66 per month).

- John's company offers matching: for every extra 1% John contributes, the company matches the 1%.

- John decides to contribute an extra £116.66 a month from his net salary. Pension contributions are taken from his gross salary, so this becomes £145.83 per month.

- That extra £145.83 is deducted from John's salary before tax is paid, which means each month John's salary only decreases by £99.16, because the government adds back 20% for basic rate tax relief (£29.16) and 12% for NI contributions (£17.50).

- The company matches this amount, so he now has £291.66 a month (£3,500 a year) extra going into his pension.

- That's a 194% return on his £99.16 that he uses to pay his future self rather than spend it today.

- John is now saving £7,000 a year, at a personal cost of just £116.66 per month.

A small sacrifice today turned into a habit over time is a simple way to set yourself up for a comfortable retirement. What's more, John's pension is invested in a sustainable and responsible way, which means he is not only securing his future prosperity but helping protect the planet at the same time.

How can I find the money to save and invest into my pension?

Lots of people say to me, 'But Rob, I can't afford to save £100 per month.' I get it. The cost of living is rising, property is becoming more expensive, and we still want to live and enjoy our lives while saving for the future. It comes back to *awareness*. If you study your payslip, follow a monthly budget, know your 'money personality' and what triggers you to spend, then you'll have a high level of self-awareness when it comes to what you can and can't afford to save into your pension. Do what you can – a little is better than nothing at all. Even the smallest action will help you accelerate towards your future self and your future goals.

If you feel you could be more financially aware, then read on. We all have money habits that we can probably improve on. For example, how many times have you walked into a supermarket and fallen victim to a 'Buy One Get One Free' (BOGOF) deal? We've all been swept away by all the 'money saving' opportunities that we see on the shelves. Buy three bottles of soft drinks for the price of two, buy one bag of salad and get another half price, buy two packets of biscuits, and get one free. . . We all know the deals that

FR££DOM: EARN IT KEEP IT GROW IT

are out there, and we all fall for them. The average person in the UK spends £1,300 more a year on these BOGOF deals than they need to (Neilan, 2016). The money you spend buying three bottles of soft drinks when you only need one is significant. These deals not only cost you dearly, but they also contribute to food waste. If you can put £20, £50 or £100 a month into a savings account or use it to top up your pension as John did, you can materially change your financial future. Absolutely everyone can change their habits in a way that will help their future selves.

Another example is adapting our spending habits to various life stages. Emily is in her early thirties and recently returned to work after maternity leave. She attended a TEDx talk that I gave in 2017 on children's pensions. In the summer of 2020, she sent me a message on Instagram:

> Hi Rob, finally sorted out my pension contributions post maternity leave and thought about your TEDx talk and what you said about ensuring our financial future. I'm not paying to commute at the moment (due to Covid) so have gifted the savings to my future self by increasing my pension contributions.

MEET YOUR FUTURE SELF

I did a quick calculation for her. The extra £175 a month that she was saving into her pension would be worth over £50,000 in ten years, and over £1,000,000 by the time she retires. This equates to her having an extra £30,000 a year in retirement, which is enough for a comfortable lifestyle when she stops work at sixty-eight. Here's how:

- Emily earns around £60,000 a year, which means she is a higher-rate taxpayer at 40%.

- Emily saves £156 a month from no longer having to commute, so she speaks to her company about contributing more into her pension.

- She paid for her travel costs from her net income, so her company adds back tax relief (40%) and NI (12%).

- This is £300 per month (£3,600 a year) of her gross salary, at a personal cost of £156.

- Emily's company matches her £300 a month or £3,600 a year of additional contributions, so she is now saving an additional £7,200 a year into her pension.

- After ten years, Emily has saved £72,000.

- If she invested in a long-term portfolio of diversified equities with a long-term growth rate of around 7%, then her pensions savings will have grown to over £100,000. (Remember, this is all at a personal 'sacrifice' of £156 per month.)

- Emily's retirement age is 68, so she has over 35 years to keep earning, keeping, and growing her money (assuming annual returns of 7%).

- After the first decade, she has over £100,000, which she leaves invested and should therefore double in the next decade.

- If she keeps up the additional contributions into her pension, after twenty years, her pension of £100,000 has doubled to £200,000 and she has saved an additional £100,000. She now has £300,000.

- In the third decade, her £300,000 doubles to £600,000 and she saves an additional £100,000. She now has £700,000.

- If she carries on for one more decade, then her pension grows to be worth over £1,500,000.

By now, you will have realised that taxes and allowances are complicated so it's worth asking your employer, 'If I increase my pension contributions, what is the maximum you will match? And if I am to increase using salary sacrifice, how much do I benefit from your employer's saving on national insurance?'

In the interest of balance, sacrificing salary for increased pension contributions carries some negative complexities. For example, your maximum mortgage borrowing may be reduced. For example, if you earn £112,000, your bank lends you £500k on a mortgage, about 4.5 times what you make. On the other hand, suppose you use salary sacrifice to save an extra £12,000 into your pension and reduce your earnings to £100,000 for tax efficiency – wise from a tax perspective to avoid the '60% tax trap'. The risk is that when you come to re-mortgage, a new lender may only lend you £450,000. This is an excellent opportunity to get financial advice and understand what's right for you.

It might surprise you to see just how much the return can be, even on a relatively small investment. This is due to three key ingredients: tax relief, employer matching and the magic of compound interest. But it also requires patience and willpower. Remember the advice of Clear: 'Changing your life is about building a positive system of habits that, when combined, deliver remarkable results.' If you keep applying this rule to managing your money, your future self will thank you. Hopefully you're beginning to see that you don't have to be a millionaire to be able to give yourself a decent retirement. You just need to understand what you should do and take some simple steps now to make it happen. Remember: awareness, action, accelerate.

Investing in your future is not just about retirement. Your day-after-tomorrow fund covers a lot more than that. Take a minute to think about what it is that you want to save for. It might be a dream holiday, yours or your children's university fees, or a big event like your wedding. You'll never save that money if you don't plan how to do it.

It's important that you have a goal, and you plan your investments around the things that you're saving for. There are always going to be bumps in the road, but if you plan properly then you can weather the rainy days and still save enough to be able to dive the Titanic in the future if you want to.

Not many people feel confident when making financial decisions or discussing things like pensions and investments. This is normal. Why should you know? It's not something that we're taught in schools, our parents are not always able to talk about it with us and it's easier to ignore than to struggle to understand something that seems complicated. However, not feeling confident should not be a reason *to do nothing*. Most of the things that I've talked about doing are simple but if you're worried or feel confused or if you have significant amount of debt that you want to clear before you start investing, you can, and should, seek professional help.

Even though I understand many of these ideas and concepts, I have a financial advisor who helps me and my family to manage my personal finances, mainly because I don't have time to make sure I am doing all the right things. The value of advice is clear – research shows that getting professional financial advice could make you £47,000 better off over the next ten years (Royal London, 2019). The nature of financial advice is evolving too: digital and Robo-Advisors mean it's now easier to access than ever.

9

Calculate Your Net Worth

'Wealth is having assets that earn while you sleep.'
— Naval Ravikant

In this chapter, I'd like to help you understand the difference between 'wealthy' and 'rich' by teaching you how to calculate your net worth. This is an important step in becoming fully aware of your financial situation, so that you can take the necessary actions to accelerate your journey towards financial freedom.

The term 'net worth' is often associated with the rich and famous, but you also have a net worth, and understanding it is crucial in creating a healthy financial future. Your net worth is the sum of how much you own, minus what you owe. It is a sign of your 'financial health'. Like going to the doctor for a physical check-up, it's important to take a deeper look into how financially solid you are beyond your current lifestyle (house, car, holidays and so on).

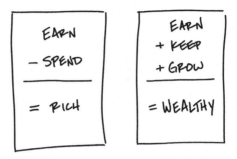

A lot of people may feel wealthy because they can afford to buy expensive things and have the lifestyle they want, but they can only afford these things because they currently earn a lot. This makes them 'rich', but are they wealthy? Being wealthy can mean not having to work and living off your assets. This is true financial freedom. It's the key to having a comfortable retirement and greater financial freedom, which links back to your overall wellbeing.

Learning how to calculate your wealth is important to ensure you're on track to enjoy a comfortable lifestyle when you retire. In the same way that understanding your payslip helps you budget for the months ahead, knowing your net worth will help you take stock of where you are in relation to long-term goals like your retirement. It helps you look at your assets holistically, so if something needs to change (like the example of Paul in a previous chapter), you can assess the impact on everything at once. In simple terms, your net wealth is the *sum of what you own, minus what you owe.*

Make a list of what you own and how much value it has:

• Your property, if you own one

• Your physical belongings like art, cars, expensive watches, furniture and luxury handbags

• Financial assets, like money in your bank, stocks and shares, ISAs, etc

• Whatever is in your various pension pots

Now make another list of what you owe and subtract this from what you own. This could include:

• Your mortgage, if you own property

• Loans, including outstanding student loans

• Any credit, such as store cards, or any outstanding balance on any of your BNPL accounts

The result is your net worth. Most people have never done this, so even just a rough estimate on the back of a napkin is a good exercise and can give a solid indication of your current financial health. The truth of the matter is, a lot of people don't know what is in their bank account right now, let alone what their assets are worth. As intimidating as it might feel, this is just a case of doing a little bit of homework, and it starts with your two lists. This exercise will also show you where you may have gaps or issues that need looking into. There are many things you can do to build your wealth and you can start at any time. It's always better late than never.

You might find that your financial health is lower than you thought after doing the 'own vs owes' calculation, but the positive to this is that once you are aware of your financial situation, you can always take actions to improve it. Someone who doesn't earn a lot can build more wealth than someone who earns twice as much. It's about making the right financial decisions over the long term. Wealth is built by the decade, not by the day, and the first step to creating it is to understand where you're at right now.

If you're thinking, 'But Rob, I can't afford to buy a house. What does this mean for my net worth?', you're not alone. It has become increasingly difficult to get a foot on the property ladder over the past ten years. The average first-time buyer is now around thirty-two years old. Home ownership among young adults has fallen dramatically, from half in 1989, to a quarter in 2016, according to the Resolution Foundation (Partington, 2018). What's driving this? Average house prices have risen by over £100,000 in the last twelve years. During that period, wages have just about kept pace with inflation, but renting has also become more expensive. This will have impacted on how much renters can save into their tomorrow fund each month. The average cost of a house deposit in the UK (excluding Greater London) is somewhere between £25,000 and £40,000, depending how much you put down. Greater London is the most expensive region for first-time buyers, with average deposits of over £100,000 (Jenkin, nd). This is a lot of money, and it's not surprising that many young people think it's out of their reach. Only fifteen local authorities in the UK offer homes that are within the affordability rules (four times the average income) (ONS, 2020). On top of all of that, the cost of living has been steadily increasing. This affects everyone but is more likely to have a disproportionate effect on younger people. A recent report by the Royal Society of Art revealed that:

- More than half of young people in work are experiencing financial precarity.

- Only a third feel that their work provides them with enough money to maintain a decent standard of living.

- Two-thirds of young people who are financially precarious are worried about their mental health and their future.

- The majority of young people do not believe they'll be able to own their own home in the future, or live a comfortable retirement (Westwater, 2022).

These are shocking statistics. It's no wonder so many young people feel frustrated when they are told by older generations to make small lifestyle changes to be able to afford a house. There's no doubt that saving for a house is a source of intergenerational tension that is damaging our ability to have valuable money conversations with our parents and loved ones. The best advice I can give anyone who relates to the challenges I've mentioned above is this: follow the principles of 'earn it, keep it, grow it' to the best of your ability. If you are saving for a deposit on your first home, consider automating your savings into a LISA. Don't try and 'keep up with the Joneses' and compare yourself to your peers. Establish those habits that will get you to your goals in a way that you can afford. If you've got your today fund, your tomorrow fund and your day-after-tomorrow fund mapped out, you can still invest. Most importantly, keep going. You've got this.

I recommend a two-stage approach when you feel ready to take steps towards growing your wealth:

1. **Start taking some small actions:** Mortgage aside, if you have debt to pay off, get this done first. If you're not in debt, think about your pension and whether you're making the most of it. Remember, company matching, and personal contributions go a long way. Remember Jess and Emily? Both have taken small actions, which they turned into ongoing habits. Jess has since paid off her store

card debt and bought her first house. Emily has made significant contributions to her pension.

2. **Be ambitious:** Once you have the basics in place, you can start to be more ambitious with your savings. This is where you might begin to grow your money by investing – which can be rewarding but should only be risked when you can afford to do so. Growing money takes time and patience, which is why it's difficult, but the difference in later years between those who play the long game and those who can't is huge. Having a plan, being prepared, and taking small and regular steps is the key to feeling confident about your finances and in control of where you're headed. When it comes to growing your wealth, there is no, 'I'll start tomorrow.'

10

Compounding Matters – Get Interested

'He who understands it, earns it; he who doesn't, pays it.'
— Albert Einstein

Growing your money is the most impactful part of your journey to financial freedom. In fact, this chapter is probably the most important chapter in this book, so I'd recommend sitting back and getting interested.

If you're new to growing your money, the thought of investing might feel intimidating, risky, or even exclusive to the 'wealthy', which is why this section of the book will teach you ways to break down barriers and manage the perceived risks associated with investing, so that you can reap the long-term rewards. One of the most helpful hacks out there when it comes to growing your money is compound interest. It's rarely talked about and taught in business school but usually forgotten by graduates.

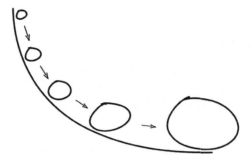

As dull as it might sound, compound interest is the secret to doubling your money every ten years, which most people with a little money that they can afford to save, can do. All you need is to have a little patience. In simple terms, compound interest means 'earning interest on your interest' and it is how Warren Buffet, who accumulated $70 billion of his $80 billion worth after he was sixty-five years old, made his money (Housel, 2020). While Buffet is clearly skilled when it comes to investing, his secret is time. He understands that to grow his money and his wealth takes time, patience and consistency.

I've already introduced you to my parents, neither of whom had high-earning jobs, but who mastered good, consistent habits with their money moves. After returning to the UK from Argentina, they were able to save their money in the bank, because the interest rates offered were an incredible 12%. This meant they could grow and double their money every six years (see table below) thanks to compound interest and the 'Rule of 72'.

The Rule of 72 is a quick, useful formula that is widely used to estimate the number of years it will take to double your invested money at a given annual rate of return.

- The Rule of 72 applies to compound interest rates on investments and on debt.

- It can be applied to anything that increases exponentially, like inflation.

- Formula: 72 ÷ rate of return = number of years to double your money.

For example, when my parents were earning 12% interest on their money, it would take them 6 years to double their money (72 ÷ 12 = 6).

If you can get a long-term investment return of 7.2% then you can double your money every 10 years (72 ÷ 7.2 = 10).

$$\frac{72}{\% \text{ RATE OF RETURN}} = \frac{\text{YEAR}}{\text{TO DOUBLE}}$$

Interest rate saving with a bank	How long to double your money?
12%	6 years
10%	7 years
7%	10 years
6%	14 years
1%	Over 70 years
0.1%	Over 700 years

Isn't that an amazing idea? For example, if someone saved £1,000 and invested it at 12% for 6 years, they would double their investment. If they invested their money at that rate for 60 years (ie, 10 times as long), they would not simply multiply their investment by 20 times (2 x 10) ie, £20,000. They would see their wealth grow to nearly £900,000 – an almost 900 times increase on their initial investment – thanks to the interest on their interest.

It is widely alleged that Albert Einstein described compound interest as 'the strongest force in the universe and the eighth wonder of the world – for he who understands it, earns it; he who doesn't, pays it.'

Another useful way to explain how compound interest works is with the game used by my educational charity, RedSTART, which asks, 'Which would you rather have: £10,000 per day for 30 days, or 1p which is doubled every day for 30 days? Work it out at ten days and decide if you want to change your mind.

How about after twenty days? And are you happy with your choice after thirty days?'

Compound interest and borrowing	
Would you rather have £10,000 per day for 30 days, or 1p that doubles every day for 30 days?	
Option 1: £10,000 per day for 30 days	Option 2: 1p that doubles every day for 30 days
After 10 days...	
£100,000	£5.12
Does anyone want to change their mind?	
After 20 days...	
£200,000	£5,243
Does anyone want to change their mind?	
After 30 days...	
£300,000	£5,368,709

Not surprisingly, most children and teachers go for £10,000 per day. It feels intuitively more than 1p doubling every day. To begin with, the £10,000 per day is the better choice. After ten days, that's the better choice, and the same goes for twenty days. That's because our brain struggles to understand exponential growth rates (1p doubling every day) vs linear ones (£10,000 per day). In fact, it takes 21 days for the 1p to double and reach £10,486, which is roughly the same as just one £10,000 per day. And it takes 26 days for the 1p doubling every day to overtake the cumulative £10,000 per day. By day 30, it's now worth £5 million, which is nearly 18 times more than £300,000. If we extend this by just one day, it's worth almost £11 million, nearly 35 times more than £310,000.

To see this in action, look back at the miracle of compounding in the table above.

Compound interest reminds me of a snowball rolling down a snow-covered hill. As the snowball rolls it picks up more snow, gaining more mass and surface area, which in turn picks up more snow, and so the snowball grows at an exponential rate. This is what happens with compound interest, but time can also be your worst enemy when it comes to being in debt. Remember Jess' story with the store card debt? If you have a store card with an APR of 29%, your debt is doubling every 2.5 years (72/29 = 2.5), ie, a £2,000 shopping spree quickly becomes a £4,000 debt. If you want to build financial resilience and avoid drowning in debt you should make paying off high interest credit and store cards your number one priority.

Building wealth and prosperity is a long-term game which requires patience. Compound interest won't get you rich quick, but it's a huge force multiplier in the long run. Start saving now and invest little and often. Don't be disheartened if you don't see results right away. (We'll also explore further ways to grow later in the text.)

11

In It To Win It

'I never attempt to make money on the stock market. I buy on the assumption that they could close the market the next day and not reopen it for ten years.'
— Warren Buffett

To grow your money over the long term, you must invest. Hold on tight though because the investment rollercoaster experiences highs and lows. In this chapter, I'll explain what investment means and how it works. By now, you're well-acquainted with examples of how others, including myself, have *earned* and *kept* money. In this chapter I'll also share a couple of stories that highlight the risks associated with *growing* your money by investing, and what happens when you panic. I'm hoping this will help you to see how investing can increase your prosperity in the future and inform you on the types of long-term decisions you might have to make for yourself along the way.

Many people put their savings into bank accounts or cash ISAs. This is partly because people don't feel comfortable about deciding where to invest, or how to invest. They also fear what will happen to their money in the event of a stock market collapse or a global financial crisis. We know that businesses go bankrupt, banks fail and investments can be lost, so it's really no wonder that people are scared to put their hard-earned money into something that looks and feels risky and volatile.

I want to make it clear that although investing might look scary up close, when we zoom out and view the stock markets from a distance, it doesn't look all that scary. When you're riding the rollercoaster itself, that first speeding descent can look terrifying from the top, but when you're back on the ground and can see the ups and downs of the whole journey, it looks a lot less daunting. In my lifetime, I've experienced several market crashes: the UK crash of 1987, the tech bubble collapse in 2000, the global financial crisis in 2008, and the 2020 Covid-19 pandemic.

Despite all of these, had you invested in 1970 and stayed firmly strapped in your seat for the duration of the ride, your investments would have grown by over 115 times in the last fifty years.

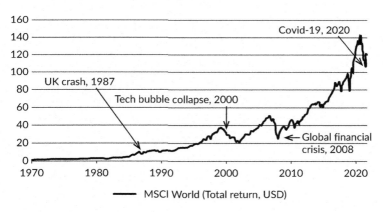

Long term growth in world equities (Source: MSCI)

Fear of market volatility is compounded by the fact that investing looks complicated and confusing. A lot of people have the impression that you need to be a maths genius to figure out how it all works. There's no denying that parts of the investment world are complex but following simple rules can help you to grow your money in a safe and responsible way.

Ultimately, over the long term, the biggest risk to your future prosperity is leaving your money in the bank. You've already met John. He's a hard worker; he contributes to his pension and he likes to save money each month. John has thought about investing some money beyond his pension contributions but doesn't know how to do it and is worried that he might lose his money if he puts it in the stock market. He's decided to play it safe and save in a regular bank account, but after twenty years, that money will be worth less than it was when he put it in the account. This is because inflation will have eroded the value of his money. If John manages to master his fears and invest his savings in a Stocks and Shares ISA, his money will go into a diversified portfolio of shares for the long term. If his investments grow at an average of 7%, then he can double his wealth every decade. In twenty years, he will have quadrupled his savings.

Over that period, he will experience ups and downs in the market. This is also known as 'volatility'. I've used the analogy of investing being like riding a rollercoaster because if you look at the chart below, the dotted line looks and feels exactly like one; from making eye-watering returns one year to gut-wrenching losses the next. The solid black line shows the same performance framed over a rolling ten-year period, which smooths out the bumps in the road. This is the return you get in decades, not days. When investing, this is the best way to grow your wealth.

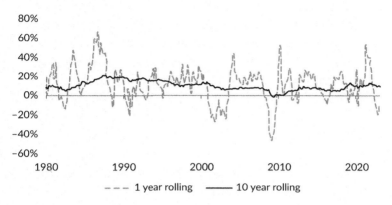

Invest for decades not days (Source: MSCI)

The hardest part of investing is getting started, and the second-hardest part is staying invested, so automating your investment – just like your savings – is the way to go. Remember, equity markets go up over the long term, so if you're just keeping your money in a regular cash savings account like John, then you are seriously limiting your financial future.

Learn from my mistakes

When the global financial crisis hit in 2008, everyone panicked and lots of people immediately took their money out of the stock market. The average person didn't start saving in the stock market again for five years, by which point it had gone up by over 50%. All those people who panicked and pulled out their money (and there were a lot of them) missed out on that return. I was one of them. Ten years later, when I saw that the investments had not only recovered, but done exceptionally well, I felt foolish. I had fallen prey to my emotions and lost out big-time. I now know that I will never make that mistake again. When the COVID-19 pandemic crashed markets in 2020, I knew to stay invested, as they would eventually recover.

Take it from me – I know how hard it is to stay steadfast during a financial panic when we're surrounded by terrifying economic forecasts and fear-mongering newspaper headlines. It's important that you try to ignore them. The story of the mythological hero, Ulysses, is a good way to remind yourself of how to act when the stock markets do get jittery. The Sirens were dangerous creatures who lured sailors to their shores with their bewitching music and enchanting singing. When sailors heard them sing, they would sail closer to the shore to get nearer to them until their ships were smashed on the rocks and they were shipwrecked and drowned. Ulysses knew of the Sirens and went to Circe for advice on what to do. She devised a plan that would allow him to hear their beautiful singing without leaving him shipwrecked. He told his oarsmen to put beeswax in their ears, to cover their eyes, and to tie him to the mast so that he could watch and listen without succumbing to the Sirens' dark magic. Because his men were blindfolded and had their ears plugged, they would row straight past the treacherous waters without hitting the rocks and being shipwrecked.

For us, the Sirens are the newspaper articles, scary headlines and financial panics. They stop us making good long-term decisions and leave us scared to invest. If we listen to them, we're in danger of shipwrecking our future prosperity. We should be aware of how the twenty-four-hour news cycle can affect how we feel about investing, and actively tune out the noise so we can stay invested and accelerate our long-term goals and objectives. To build long-term wealth, we need to save regularly and to grow our money we need to take smart risks and invest it. Keeping our savings in the bank is a bad idea over the long term as it won't beat inflation. To beat inflation, we need to invest in a diversified portfolio of equities, bonds and properties. The challenge with investing is that it is a rollercoaster ride, but if we can be like Ulysses and stay the course, we can grow our money – and even enjoy the ride.

When investing, it's essential to differentiate between short-term noise and long-term market trends. Short-term noise refers to the day-to-day market fluctuations often driven by short-term events, such as company earnings reports, geo-political news such as the Russia-Ukraine war, inflation, and interest rates. These market moves can be challenging to predict and cause short-term market volatility, ie, the call of the 'Sirens'. The key to growing your money is benefiting from the long-term market trends over decades.

These trends are often driven by broader economic and social factors such as demographic shifts, technological advancements, and macroeconomic policies. The charts below show long-term growth from investing in world equities from 1970 to the end of 2022. Over this period, if you invested £1,000, it would now be worth over £115,000 at the end of 2022. That's a rate of return of nearly 10% a year over the last 50 years, doubling your money every seven years. However, when we look at the short-term noise of investing in markets, it can feel scary. During the global financial crisis (2008/09), world equities fell by nearly 25% in one day. During the COVID-19 pandemic (2020/21), they fell by over 15% in one day. When your investments drop like this, particularly over one day, it can be as gut-wrenching and terrifying as a rollercoaster's first speeding descent. The downward trajectory is rapid, and that panic might make you want to get off the ride. However, it takes courage to stay the course. Though passengers riding the investment rollercoaster can expect sharp turns and sudden changes in direction, the most sensible choice you can make is to ride it out until the end. These charts prove that long-term investment does take an upward trajectory, so you need to be like Ulysses and zoom out to see the long-term trend. When you look at the average return over 'decades, not days', it averages about 10%, with the lowest return from 2000 to 2010.

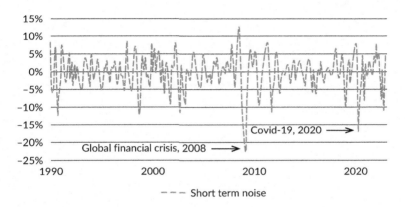

Beware the Sirens (Source: MSCI)

When investing, it's essential to focus on long-term trends (decades) rather than short-term noise (days). Short-term fluctuations can distract and cause panic, leading to hasty and potentially harmful investment decisions. Instead, by investing in world equities for decades not days, you can align with your long-term goals and hold steady like Ulysses through the short-term noise of the Sirens.

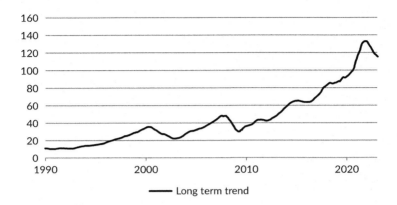

Be like Ulysses (Source: MSCI)

12

Diversify

'Victory awaits him who has everything in order.
Luck some people call it.'
— Roald Amundsen

W e've covered *why* you should invest, and in this chapter, I'm going to talk about *how* you should invest, and why it's important to diversify your investments. It's important to understand the difference between speculating and investing. They are very different and shouldn't be confused.

Speculating

This is where you think about the stock market every day and go into your daily trading account wanting to buy or sell shares depending on what's happening with their share prices. If you're looking to buy shares and sell them in a couple of weeks, then the chances are that you're speculating.

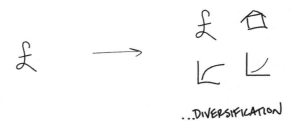

...DIVERSIFICATION

I would warn against doing this unless you have spare money that you don't mind losing, and you really know what you're doing. The apps are designed to make it look easy and almost like a game, but speculating is risky. The rewards can be high, but you could also end up losing everything. In fact, if you go on the homepage of any online trading platform in the UK, they carry a warning on how many clients lose money. For example, seven out of ten retail investor accounts lose money when trading CFDs on eToro (CMC Markets, 2021). (A CFD is a financial contract that pays the differences in the settlement price between the open and closing trades.)

The pandemic created a new wave of speculators. These people were driven by the hope of getting rich quick – the call of the Sirens! The 'Zoom Boom' saw many speculators buy shares in the likes of Peloton and Zoom, assuming the prices would continue to go up because they were popular at the time, but they didn't. Anyone who borrowed to speculate could now be in serious trouble.

Investing

This is when you recognise that you don't know what the future holds, but you want to hold shares and participate in long-term economic growth. Warren Buffett, one of the richest men in the world, is an investor, not a speculator. He's not betting on what will happen to the S&P 500 next week, or what will happen to the price of Apple shares. Instead, he's looking to the long term and deciding which companies he wants to own (have shares in) ten years from now. If you want to secure your future financial wellbeing, it's best to take the long-term approach. You can do this by following the Amundsen method, which we'll come to later in this chapter.

How to diversify

When you invest for the long term, you'll be investing your money for decades. It doesn't really matter how your stocks and shares are performing on a day-to-day basis. Instead of betting on one or two companies 'being the future', when you spread your investments by investing in many ways, you are giving yourself several different ways to grow your money. Spreading your bets also reduces the risk of losing everything. You'll have heard of the saying, 'Don't put all your eggs in one basket.' This applies to investments. Professional investors call this *diversification*, which is the best way to smooth out those investment bumps in the road.

If all your wealth is tied up in one company, you're at risk. We see this happen a lot with people who work at a company and who are given shares as a reward for their service. Usually, the more senior you are, the larger proportion of your compensation is paid in stocks. It's never a diversified basket of stocks, usually just the stock of the company that you work for. The same goes for entrepreneurs, who invest a lot of time, energy and money into their business. They often have a lot of their money tied up, so they are not diversified, and they are taking a big risk.

When I started my career in investment banking, part of my bonus was paid in shares. When the business was doing really well, my shares did well, but when the opposite happened and the business did not do as well, my shares fell in value. For some employees, this can have catastrophic implications. You might remember the company 'WeWork'. Employees were given lots of shares and stock options. On paper these looked to be worth a lot of money, but when the business collapsed, those shares became worthless (Sainato, 2019). If all your wealth is predicated on the success of a single stock or a single thing, you're not diversified. When it comes to making sure that you have enough money for when you retire, you need to spread your risk, because the truth is, we just don't know what's going to happen in the future. The only thing we can be certain of is uncertainty.

When you're investing for the long term, you need to reduce your risk by investing not just in different businesses, but also in different countries. This all helps to further spread the risk of your investments. If you live in the UK, the common thing to do is to invest in the UK stock market. It's close to home and feels familiar, so why not? The UK makes up less than 4% of the world's market capitalisation, which means that it's only a tiny part of the investment universe. America makes up nearly 60% (Statista, 2022). If I said to you, 'Look, here are all the shares in the world, where do you want to invest?', would you put all your money in a tiny 4%? Probably not. You want to be exposed to different areas so you can have the opportunity to grow your money by investing in a variety of different countries and companies. Some of the largest companies in the US (Apple and Microsoft, for example) are worth trillions of dollars (Finbox, 2022). For example, if Apple was to spin off AirPods as a stand-alone company, it would be the biggest company in the UK. Microsoft is worth more than the hundred biggest companies in the UK combined. You can see why it makes sense to diversify and invest in countries other than the UK. None of us can predict which countries will be successful in the future. Before the Great Depression of the 1930s, Argentina was among the ten richest economies in the world – a far cry from today. Therefore, global diversification is important: it spreads the risk, and it increases your opportunities for prosperity.

The same goes for companies. No one knows which sectors are going to be the heroes of the future. The story of the last decade has all been about technology and what we call the FAANGS (Facebook, Apple, Amazon, Netflix, Google and a couple of others). No one could have predicted this happening thirty years ago and no one can predict what business will look like thirty years from now. The only thing that we can count on is that over time countries grow, economies grow and companies grow, and so if you own a small amount of assets in all of these, you will benefit from that overall growth. However, individual companies and economies can fall, which is why diversification matters.

I've talked about investing in stocks and shares. Another way to invest is in bonds, which are effectively a way of lending. Governments and companies use bonds to borrow money. Bonds have a lower rate of return, but generally speaking, they're also less risky. When the markets are bumpy and everyone's worried about what might happen to the economy in the short term, government bonds tend to go up in value, because they're thought of as safe assets.

The other major asset class that people invest in is property. That might include offices, retail stores and data warehouses. Property is a good long-term investment, but as with all investments, it's important that you know exactly what you're investing in and consider any risk.

How much do I invest, and where?

You have some money to invest, and you know you need to invest it wisely. Stocks and Shares ISAs allow you to invest in a lot of different things at once rather than buying lots of individual investments. There are other options, but we'll stick to a Stocks and Shares ISA for now.

Which one do you choose? Stocks and Shares ISAs will tend to have different risk ratings. This means that they invest in a different combination of equities, bonds and property, so you can manage how much risk you are taking. Bonds are less risky than equities, so if you want less risk, you tend to have more bonds and fewer equities.

The rule of thumb used to be that if you're investing for the long term, you take 100 and subtract your age to calculate how much you should invest in equities. I'm in my early forties and should have about 60% of my day-after-tomorrow fund invested in equities, and then the rest in bonds and property. But like Captain Tom, we're all living longer. To compensate for that, you will need to start with 120 and subtract your current age. For me, this means I should invest about 80% of my long-term money in global equities and the other 20% in bonds and property.

When I've done that, I can sit back and let my investments do their job. I know that my investment strategy is high-risk in the short term, because equities tend to move up and down over this time, but in the long term it'll give me the best opportunity and the greatest amount of financial wellbeing. I'm going to be like Ulysses and ignore the Sirens, row past all those terrifying headlines and stay strapped into my seat on the investment rollercoaster. The day-to-day changes in the stock market are not going to affect my money if it's held for decades, not days.

What we can learn from #TheAmundsenMethod

Before I began working in finance, I wanted to be a glaciologist. I studied glaciers at university and was fascinated by them. I love mountains and anything to do with polar exploration. I want to tell you the story of Robert Falcon Scott and Roald Amundsen, who raced to be the first to the South Pole in 1911. Though different versions of this story have been shared over the years, I am going to share the version I was first introduced to, as it gives us a relevant insight into how we should look after our investments. While saving for your future might not be as dramatic as an Antarctic race, it has many of the same features. You need to have a plan, save every year in a disciplined way, and prepare for the unexpected.

Scott, a British naval officer, and Amundsen, a Norwegian explorer, approached the race in very different ways. Amundsen had wanted to be an Arctic explorer from a young age – apparently as a boy he'd slept with the windows open every night so that his body would get used to the cold. He'd clearly been preparing for a life of polar exploration for a long time. Between 1903 and 1905, Amundsen went to live with the local Inuit peoples, where he learned how to survive in the Arctic conditions. He looked at how they used sleds and dogs, he looked at the furs they wore, and he trained both himself and his men to live as they did. He took only a small team with him to the South Pole and had a disciplined plan that he stuck to. Each man carried his own supplies on lightweight sleds that were pulled by dogs. Amundsen also set up kites on the sleds that would pull them along when it was windy, to help out the dogs and increase their speed. Amundsen also had a plan that he stuck to. Whether it was good weather or bad, he would stick to his plan.

Scott, on the other hand, acted differently. He took mechanical snow machines which looked impressive but had never been tested in Arctic conditions. He also took ponies, masses of supplies and a few dogs. Scott didn't have a plan, and so on a good day when the weather was fine, he would march forty miles, but on a day when the weather was bad, they would all stay in their tents and Scott would write in his diary. Their progress was haphazard, and Scott's men ended up exhausted from trying to do too many miles in a single day and not having enough time to rest.

How does this story relate to financial wellbeing? It's clear that Amundsen had a disciplined plan, and that sticking to it was a big part of his success. He was operating in 'power-saving mode'. The incredible thing with Amundsen is that he travelled all the way to the South Pole and got back a few days earlier than he predicted he would. Scott got to the South Pole late, and, tragically, he and all of his men died on the way back. Amundsen knew he needed to keep his men fit and healthy, and he didn't want to push his men too hard on the good days. They could easily have done more, but instead they rested, checked their supplies, and made sure that everyone was fit and mentally well enough to continue the journey the next day. When Scott was in his tent and not moving at all due to the bad weather, Amundsen and his team were marching on slowly. It might have taken them the whole day, but they did it. Even when the South Pole was in sight, they stuck to the same pace instead of speeding up.

When Amundsen finally got to the Pole, he put up his camp, took some samples, took some photographs, and then started on the return journey. When he went back, he followed the same method. This is a great example of an atomic habit: he was consistent, and he and his men reaped the rewards of that forward planning and that consistency. Scott and all his men died before they reached their base camp. They were ill-prepared, malnourished and exhausted, whereas every single one of Amundsen's men made it back alive, and astonishingly, had even gained weight during their expedition.

The point is that Scott and Amundsen experienced exactly the same weather, exactly the same terrain and exactly the same external conditions. It was the decisions they made that led to their success or failure, not any external factors – a bit like Jane and her friend, who started their careers at the same time, on similar salaries and with similar outgoings, but due to making different financial decisions, ended up in different financial situations.

Think about the way that you invest. It's not a good idea for your future to invest a large sum into your ISA and pension one year, and then nothing the next.

This is like what Scott did and it didn't help him in the long run. *Be like Amundsen and put in a steady amount every month.* It's this method that will preserve your financial resilience in the short term and build long-term financial wellbeing. Slow and steady always wins the race. There will be good years and bad years, but you need to keep on investing. Make sure that you save every month, even if it's only a small amount. Doing this will ensure your journey to future freedom in the same way that Amundsen's tactics helped him achieve his goal of reaching the South Pole.

13

Invest Responsibly

'If working apart we are a force powerful enough to destabilise our planet, surely working together we are powerful enough to save it. In my lifetime I've witnessed a terrible decline. In yours, you could – and should – see a wonderful recovery.'
   — David Attenborough's opening speech at
      COP26 in Glasgow

I was born in Holland and have two strong memories from this time: one is of ice-skating on the canals at Christmas time (something you sadly can't do anymore, because of climate change). The second is knowing that I was born below sea-level, which gave me a real sense, even as a child, that the place where I was living was particularly vulnerable to sea levels rising. When I left university, I was offered the opportunity to study the impact of deglaciation on the Hindu Kush mountains in Northern Pakistan, an amazing experience before embarking on my career in finance. I've no doubt that in a different world, I'd be a professor of glaciology and probably be in Antarctica studying the impact of climate change on our melting icecaps. My love of glaciers remains close to my heart. My work in finance means that, ironically, I have a chance to fight against climate change just as effectively as if I were a scientist in the Antarctic.

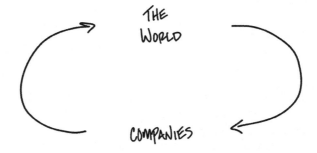

In this chapter we are going to start exploring the idea that your money can be a *force for good*, so that you're not just growing your money for your own prosperity – you're also doing so for the prosperity of the planet and the people who live on it. It's tempting to look at the world and think, 'I can't change all of this,' but even as individuals, we can have a big impact in changing the prosperity of the planet by being aware of how and where we invest our money.

In 2021, public concern for the environment reached a 'historically high level', with a third of UK adults claiming that climate change was their second-biggest concern for the country after the pandemic (Ipsos, 2021). These concerns are not unfounded: in my lifetime, the global population nearly doubled from 4 billion to 8 billion, carbon dioxide in the atmosphere increased by nearly a quarter, and remaining wilderness has decreased by over a third. We are changing our planet at an alarming rate, and if we continue to push the earth's boundaries by consuming, spending, investing and doing business in the way we have been, there will be no planet left. The good news is that, just like it's never too late to reverse your financial situation, it's also not too late to reverse the damage we are doing to the planet. However, it is essential that we act now.

For many countries, we live in an economic system known as capitalism. Capitalism has always been about accumulating savings, spending them on products or investing them in businesses, and generating profit that drives economic growth. These profits create more money that can then be re-invested in the system. There's nothing inherently wrong with this, but over time, profit and consumption have become more important than anything else, without accounting for negative impacts such as pollution or destruction of wildlife.

In the 1950s and 1960s, businesses generally used to be more well-rounded and were run in a more sustainable way. What happened? In the 1970s and 1980s, a new doctrine emerged, championed by the economist Milton Friedman. In an essay titled 'The Social Responsibility of Business is to Increase its Profits' published in *The New York Times* Magazine, September 13, 1970, he argued that the sole purpose of a business was to generate profit for the shareholders (Friedman, 1970). As a result, capitalism became all about shareholders. It was the gradual beginning of a world economic system that now operates in a framework focused primarily on profit, with little regard for the impact on people or the planet.

What's clear is we need to move away from a *take, make, waste* model to a circular economy of *recycle, reuse, remake*. We need to stop seeing sustainable choices as sacrifices and move to a way of working where capitalism is done well, and shareholders engage with businesses to raise industry standards and make every company better. I'd like to tell you two stories that show how capitalism is beginning to shift towards being more responsible. In 2016, world-renowned San Francisco 49ers quarterback Colin Kaepernick took a stand against racism and police brutality. At the start of a nationally televised game, he knelt while the national anthem was playing. More and more players started to do the same, and some called for the protesting players to be fired. By 2018, the nation was divided because of increased racism, police brutality and social injustice, with the black community feeling oppressed and helpless due to repeated incidents across the country.

Nike launched its thirtieth anniversary 'Just Do It' campaign with a poignant and beautifully shot advert featuring Colin Kaepernick. The advertisement image began with a quote that stated 'Believe in something. Even if it means sacrificing everything' (Burns, 2018). By showing support for black communities, athletes and civil rights activists, Nike drew a great deal of attention with their new campaign. It polarised its consumer base. Nike proceeded with the campaign to bring attention to the issues the people in the campaign were facing, and the brand's support. This is a great example of social governance from a big brand done exceptionally well. Not only did Nike speak up for minority communities, but it demonstrated its values to consumers and shareholders.

Despite the backlash to the campaign, Nike reported a 31% sales increase over the Labour Day weekend alone (Martinez, 2018). Five years on, share prices have more than doubled and, at the same time, Nike has been a leading brand in embracing the move to a circular economy, with more of its products being made from recycled materials. I think this is a great example of being a good ancestor to people and planet.

Around the same time as the Nike campaign, car maker Volkswagen was discovered to be manipulating the way that they measured their emissions. They systematically installed software aimed at cheating on emissions tests on 11 million diesel vehicles around the world – actively engaging in a strategy of fraud to deceive customers and regulators alike. Its actions resulted in nitrogen oxide emissions up to forty times the legal limit, producing an estimated 46,000 tons of pollution between 2008 and 2015 – a clear negative impact on the environment. Shareholders' judgement of this move was evident from the immediate market reaction, which saw the share price drop by a third, wiping billions from VW's value. In the case of #Dieselgate, VW's efforts were focused on short-term profit, rather than aligned with long-term responsible and sustainable growth (EPA, 2021).

What's most interesting about #Dieselgate is the 'turnaround' story which followed. While shares in VW fell by around 30% in one day, since the scandal, the car manufacturer has managed to recover by readjusting its way of operating. With the executive board responsible for #Dieselgate fired and new leadership in place, bringing with it a new culture and new ways of working, VW has moved from producing internal combustion engines and to being one of the world's largest manufacturers of electric vehicles, proving the power of engaging businesses to do better.

Just like we need to build up our own financial resilience to weather storms on the bumpy road, being a responsible business is also about resilience. Businesses with a focus on sustainable revenues can survive shocks, whether from financial crises or natural disasters, because their resilience comes from relationships with their employees, their communities and the environment.

Investors can influence how companies operate, and broader economic systems, by being aware of where their money is invested and actively choosing where to put their money. One way of doing this is by investing in companies with high Environmental, Social and Governance standards (or ESG, as the industry refers to them). It's not just about the pure financial metrics of revenues, costs and profits, but looking outwards at impact that the company has on the rest of the world.

With climate change on more people's agenda, the environmental impact of how a business operates – such as greenhouse gas emissions or impact on climate change – tends to take the ESG spotlight, which we will go into in more detail in the next chapter. However, social impact – such as employee conditions, diversity and how a business interacts with its communities – and governance – how tax is managed, board structure, bribery and corruption – are also essential to how a business operates, manages and interacts with people and planet.

If a business is producing renewable energy, then that company is having a positive impact in the world. Responsible investing is about engaging businesses, all businesses and not just oil and gas, to be better and to look after people and planet, long term. The good news is that we can all do our bit to redress this balance, and in the next chapter I am going to explain how, by investing and thanks to the power of your pension, you can use your money as a force for good.

14

Your Money As
A Force For Good

'The returns we need can only come from a system
that works, the benefits we pay are worth more in a
world worth living in.'
— CEO of a Dutch Pension Fund

If the 2010s were about digitalisation, then the 2020s
will be about decarbonisation. In this chapter, we
will focus in more detail on the *E* of ESG and delve
a little deeper into the transition to net-zero, how we
can get there, and how decarbonising your investments can benefit the prosperity of the planet.

We know that we can no longer afford to not act. It is
our collective responsibility to reverse climate change.
Where possible, I make sustainable personal, business
and investment choices that take a long-term approach

to my own prosperity and the future prosperity of the planet. In 2021, Redington, the company I co-founded with Dawid Konotey Ahulu, completely offset all its carbon emissions since launching. How did we do it? We calculated the company's cumulative carbon emissions since it was founded and completely off-set this amount by investing in five natural capital projects around the world. These included peatland restoration and conservation in Indonesia and forest protection in Colombia. By doing this, Redington has become 'climate positive' by removing more CO_2 from the atmosphere than it has produced.

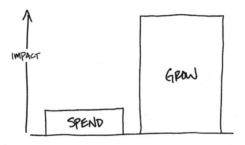

I try to eat less red meat, drive an electric car, and use 100% renewable electricity at home. I've managed to make my own investment portfolio and pension carbon-neutral. I've done this without 'divesting', which means avoiding companies that are bad for the planet. Anyone can divest to make their portfolio as carbon-neutral as possible, which is the investment equivalent of dumping your rubbish in your neighbours' garden to feel better about the state of your own. It doesn't solve the problem and the rubbish still exists. You can, however, 'engage' with companies. Engagement is influencing companies to make positive changes and better choices for the benefit of the planet.

My friend Tara is co-founder of 'Best Intentions', a great personal finance blog. Tara shares my mission to empower everyone to achieve financial wellbeing. She believes that where you earn your money, where you save your money, where you spend your money and where you invest your money *all* have an impact on the world. Where you *earn* your money relates to your employer and whether they operate as a responsible business. Where you *keep* (save) your money relates to who you bank with. Perhaps you've never considered whether your bank is committed to transitioning to net-zero, but now would be the time to find out and decide if you're aligned with the steps they are taking to become better ancestors. Where you *spend* your money is the conscious choices you make every day as a consumer. And where you *grow* (invest) your money relates to whether you are investing in a responsible way.

It comes back to awareness: once you understand the impact of your money on the planet, you can take action to make sure it's positive and accelerate the transition to net-zero. We are waking up to the fact that we can make a monumental difference by changing our investment strategies to those that are aligned with the future prosperity of the planet and the people living on it.

If you're passionate about shaping the world through your investments, you can start to move beyond investing in a sustainable and responsible way and start thinking about focused investment in new innovations and technologies which will accelerate progress to a more sustainable future. One such area is food production. Did you know that agriculture is responsible for 25% of the world's CO_2 emissions (Ritchie, 2019)? A lot of the way our food is harvested and processed is not only bad for us as humans, but also bad for the environment. By thinking about how, and where, you invest your money, and then investing in companies and businesses that produce food in a more sustainable way, you can help create a better future for everyone.

Four steps towards sustainable investment choices

You can make sustainable investment choices by following these four steps:

1. **Step one: Assess the carbon footprint of your pension and investment portfolio.** Ask the company you invest with about the carbon intensity of your portfolio. This is information they should have and should be sharing with you as part of the ongoing performance of your investments, including your pension. The good news is that many of the UK's largest pension

providers have committed to be 'net-zero' by 2050 and have a roadmap to decarbonise their portfolios with science-based targets for how they are going to achieve that commitment, every five years (Gov.uk, 2021). If you are self-employed, you might also want to pick a pension that is aligned to net-zero and has a clear plan on how to get there.

- **Effort:** Easy

- **Impact:** High (due to the size and scale of our collective pensions)

- **Risk:** Low

2. **Step two: Engage to be aligned with net-zero.** Now that you know the difference between engagement and divestment and how to have a say in where your money is being invested, you can also find out if your money is being used to engage companies which emit the most CO_2 to change their ways of working and do better. What if your money engaged:

- Every oil and gas company to transition to net-zero

- Every auto-manufacturer to switch to making electric vehicles

- Those electric vehicles to be made using the principles of the circular economy (something that BMW is now doing)

- All businesses to focus on sustainable revenues, rather than just revenues

Of the thousands of companies there are in the world, just 100 companies (including BP, ExxonMobil and Shell) are accountable for over 70% of the world's carbon emissions (CDP, 2017). Engaging the hundred biggest CO_2-emitting culprits to do better is one of the most effective things you can do to help us reach net-zero. There are pension providers out there who have divested from these 100 companies along with offering 'fossil-fuel free' portfolios. Choosing one might feel like a responsible choice, but as I've explained, divestment really doesn't solve the problem as effectively as engaging with the largest CO_2-emitting companies – and that's across all industries, not just oil and gas. The best way to see if your investments are engaging with companies is to check if the company you invest with is a member of 'Climate Action 100+'. Ask them to give an example as to how they have engaged with these companies in the last twelve months, so you know they're walking the walk and doing what they claim.

- **Effort:** Easy

- **Impact:** High (due to the size and scale of our collective pensions)

- **Risk:** Low

3. **Step three: Invest in carbon credits.** By now you should know the carbon intensity of your pension and investments, and whether that was achieved through engagement. If you can afford it, consider going one step further and purchasing

carbon credits. For example, I calculated the carbon intensity of all my investments and have purchased carbon credits (EU emissions trading system) to offset these emissions. Buying carbon credits doesn't remove CO_2 from the environment like the natural capital projects do. However, it does push up the price for emitting CO_2 to change businesses' behaviour for the better. This should only be a small portion of your overall investments. They are volatile and a little like buying a single stock (and remember you need to be diversified as an investor).

- **Effort:** Medium

- **Impact:** Medium (it impacts the transition to net-zero, but it makes emitting carbon more expensive for businesses and so changes behaviours)

- **Risk:** Medium

4. **Step four: Invest in businesses driving change.** You can go even further by researching and investing in the most game-changing startups, dedicated to helping the world reach net-zero. It's important to remember that because these businesses are startups, they are a lot riskier than the big companies that will make up your pension portfolio. Around 50% of all startups and small businesses fail in their first five years (BLS, Table 7) – so only invest money you are willing to lose. When I invest in businesses like these, I like to use Enterprise

FR££DOM: EARN IT KEEP IT GROW IT

Investment Schemes. They are tax-efficient and help manage the risks associated with startups.

I choose to invest in businesses focused on addressing climate change and biodiversity because I am passionate about what they do. I understand the risks, which is why they are a small portion of my whole investment portfolio. If these businesses go bankrupt, I can claim some money back through tax wrappers, so my future financial wellbeing is not being put at risk.

- **Effort:** High

- **Impact:** Medium (high if these startups are successful)

- **Risk:** High

It's clear that in the next decade we need to accelerate the move to a circular economy of recycle, reuse, remake. The automobile and steel industries are already starting to do this, transitioning from traditional capitalism to capitalism with impact (tackling the United Nations sustainable development goals) where shareholders engage with businesses to raise industry standards and make every company better.

When it comes to decarbonising your financial footprint, what's most exciting is that the technology to help the world decarbonise already exists. Now is the time to participate in the action. If you want to find out more about the role of finance and business when addressing the issue of climate change, I'd recommend watching two game-changing documentaries: 'Breaking Boundaries' and the World Wildlife Fund's (WWF) 'Our Planet: Too Big to Fail'.

Investing your pension as a force for good

Your pension is a particularly good way of making your money a force for good. The money in UK pensions is worth trillions of pounds. Your workplace pension will have billions per year to invest. This is used by companies and industries to keep innovating, expanding, hiring and prospering, which is why how you invest your money has the potential to be a catalyst for change. As we know, pension contributions normally come from three sources: the government (your State Pension), your employer, and yourself (via your personal contributions). Regardless as to how you're currently topping up your pension, and even if you're close to retirement, it's likely you haven't engaged with where that money is going, because you probably don't think of it as 'your money'.

Think back to the chapter where you met your future self and learned that investing in your pension was 'moving' money. Just because you've moved that money and are not spending it in the traditional sense today, that doesn't mean it's not currently being used on your behalf. Until you engage with where that money is going, those decisions are being made by other people (fund managers) who decide which companies or industries need that investment – usually by buying shares and bonds in those companies to grow your money. Your money is likely to be spread across diverse industries such as renewable energy and technology, as well as well-known businesses like Disney, Google and Unilever. They all need this money to grow their revenues sustainably in the future by shifting to a circular economy.

Investing your pension responsibly doesn't mean that you compromise the financial performance of your investment. A couple of years ago, I spoke to a Dutch pension fund manager, who said, 'The returns we need can only come from a system that works. The benefits we pay are worth more in a world worth living in.' He recognised that although it was his job to invest billions of euros for the millions of members in his pension fund, it's about much more than that. The way we make money matters. If the way that we make that money means that Holland (where I was born) is completely flooded and the city of Amsterdam is under water, if it means that we lose our wildlife or we can't grow food and millions of people are displaced, then what kind of future are we investing for?

How you invest your money has the potential to be a catalyst for change. In fact, ensuring that your pension contribution is being invested responsibly – that good habit over an average forty-year career – is twenty-seven times more impactful than flying less, eating less read meat, and cycling to work (though we should all make an effort to do those things as well). When it comes to using money as a force for good, we do need companies to act responsibly and operate more sustainably. But it is not only the big, but bold moves also made by businesses that will drive the change we need; it is in the thousands of steps taken by all of us together. We might look at the world and feel helpless, or that we have no voice, but the truth is we can dramatically change the planet's prosperity simply by thinking about how we earn, keep and grow our money.

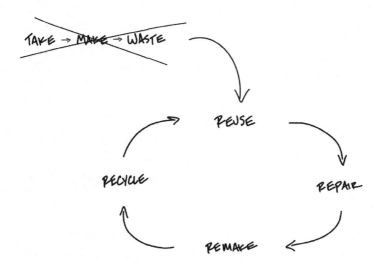

A note on cryptocurrencies before we dive into chapters 15 and 16

I began writing FR££DOM at the start of lockdown 2020, and the three years since saw us live through some unpredictable changes in our economy – most recently with the cost-of-living crisis and rising inflation. Witnessing these financial fluctuations has provided an interesting opportunity to verify the advice offered throughout the book; none of which has been more prevalent than with the following two chapters on cryptocurrencies.

Editing the chapters on cryptocurrency has been against a volatile and uncertain backdrop in this space. We have seen Bitcoin fall by nearly 70% since the start of the year, 'stablecoins', created to mitigate volatility in the crypto space, collapse and FTX, the world's third largest crypto exchange, went bust after turning out to be one of the most prominent fraud cases in finance ever.

A salient and reassuring takeaway has been that while cryptocurrencies remain a fast-evolving and unpredictable asset class, my approach to investing in the digital asset space remains the same.

Yes, I am among those who have lost value in my investments in cryptocurrencies. Still, I remain invested regardless because my investment approach is decades, not days. So I invested what I could afford to lose and diversified across the cryptocurrencies that I best understood – ie, not speculation.

For you as the reader, it will be interesting to see how the cryptocurrency markets have evolved when you read this. If you choose to participate in the space, the tools in the following two chapters will enable you to do so more confidently.

15

The Crypto Conundrum

'With a track record going back over a decade, cryptocurrencies are clearly more than just a fad. But they remain widely misunderstood by many people, with doubts persisting about their genuine value and practical use. Investment in any crypto asset is speculative and your capital is at risk, if you invest in crypto, be prepared to lose your money.'
— *Forbes*, July 2022

It would be strange to write a book about money without the inclusion of its digital counterpart, cryptocurrency. (When referencing 'crypto' throughout the next two chapters, I am using the word as an umbrella term to cover everything from Bitcoin and Ethereum to blockchain, cryptocurrencies, Non-Fungible Tokens (NFTs), tokenisation, the blockchain, web 3.0 – and everything else in this space.) But how does crypto, and other digital assets, slot into your financial future? Specifically, should they, or can they, help you grow your money?

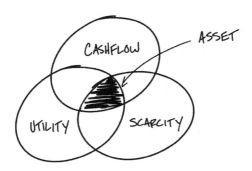

At the end of 2022, despite the volatility of the market, the original cryptocurrency, Bitcoin, remains the most popular and largest cryptocurrency in the world. Like riding the equity investment rollercoaster, investing in Bitcoin has been wild. At the start of 2017 you could buy a single Bitcoin for less than $1,000; its value shot up to nearly $20,000 at the end of that year. In 2018 it fell by almost 80% before another meteoric ride up to $60,000 in March 2021. It fell back and then reached $60,000 again in November 2021. At the end of 2022, its value has fallen by nearly 70% to $17,000. One thing for sure is that investing in this space is volatile and requires discipline. You will definitely need to channel your inner Amundsen.

What is crypto?

Cryptocurrency is a decentralised digital asset or digital form of money built on blockchain technology. The power of decentralised finance (DeFi) is that using blockchain, or distributed ledger technology, allows individuals to record ownership of assets, and verify and track them through time. What makes me excited about DeFi is that cryptography protects against counterfeiting. The fact that it's public means that it's not controlled by the government – or anyone. In fact, it's controlled by everyone. The fact that crypto is digital means that anyone who can access the internet can be in this space. On a more philosophical level, you could argue that crypto offers an inclusive and empowering future for finance, where everyone on the planet can access, buy and sell assets. DeFi has the potential to change and disrupt the financial services industry, but it raises more than a few questions:

- Will DeFi's trust-based, transparent transactions on the blockchain make the financial market more accessible to everyone?
- How will customers, users and investors benefit?
- How will this fit into our financial wellbeing?

Before you consider investing in cryptocurrency, which is currently unregulated, it's vital to be aware of the debate surrounding it and the potential risks and benefits. In a speech at the Peterson Institute for International Economics, the Financial Conduct Authority (FCA) Chief Executive Nikhil Rathi talked of the benefits of the US and UK working together regarding cryptocurrency, including stablecoins and the exploration of central bank digital currencies. The UK, US and Singapore also announced the launch of the International Organization of Securities Commissions (IOSCO) taskforce on decentralised finance and crypto market integrity risks. The FCA will lead on crypto assets, and the US Securities and Exchange Commission will focus on DeFi. Let's look at the two main sides.

Heads: On one side, there are those who wouldn't touch the digital money space with a bargepole. They consider crypto the tech-based 'tulip bubble' of our time, offering no intrinsic value, and, worst of all, facilitating criminal activity. They think that speculation (rather than sound investment) will drive up the value of digital money to an extreme, before eventually crashing the market.

Tails: On the other side of the coin are those who think that crypto is the currency of the future, set to replace the US dollar as the currency of the world, with DeFi offering the promise to transform finance in the way we move money, buy, sell, invest and verify transactions.

I've been investing in digital assets (crypto) and companies involved in DeFi for a while now and take a balanced view on the digital asset spectrum. My approach isn't to 'get rich quick', but more to strike a balance between participating in as much of the space as I understand and including digital assets in my diversified investment portfolio, so that I'm neither left behind should the asset class succeed, nor left exposed should it crash. I'm going to show you how you, too, can take this approach, by applying the Amundsen method that we explored earlier. Like exploring Antarctica, setting off into the unchartered territory of cryptocurrency will only be supportive of your long-term financial wellbeing if you're prepared for the expedition ahead. If the world of DeFi is unknown terrain to you, you might want to consider taking the following five steps.

1. Invest in what you understand

If the fear of missing out (FOMO) has encouraged you to jump on the crypto bandwagon, remember Ulysses and the call of the Sirens. Just as I've cautioned against succumbing to the headlines and pulling your investments as soon as the stocks are down, the same remains true when it comes to letting the Sirens seduce you with the ideology that crypto is a sure-fire way to get rich quick. While many investors (and speculators) have been successful in investing in digital money, cryptocurrency is not a shortcut to long-term financial wellbeing. Those 'cryptomillionaires' (along with anyone you know who has had a bit of luck with crypto and likes to share their success) are the Sirens. They're everywhere. You're probably used to overhearing them in restaurants, count them among your friends and family – and no dinner party is complete without one – so beware their call.

Like Amundsen educated himself ahead of his expedition to the South Pole, the best results from investing in crypto come from understanding what lies ahead in this space, and having a long-term, sustainable plan such as 'buying to own in ten years' rather than 'buying to sell next week.' If you don't understand what crypto is, how the blockchain works, or concepts such as 'proof of work' versus 'proof of stake', what 'mining' is, what 'hash rates' are, or the difference between Bitcoin or Ethereum, then the chances are you don't really understand crypto. If you're not investing in what you understand, then you are, in fact, speculating – hoping to get rich quick – which seldom works. Remember, it's better to be prepared and take small steps rather than rush into something you're not equipped for.

2. Find an Inuit

To understand what you're getting yourself into with your crypto investments, and to ensure you're prepared for setbacks along the way, the best thing you can do is educate yourself on the space, by applying #TheAmundsenMethod and seeking advice. I've mentioned that I invest in digital assets, but at this stage in my long-term crypto journey I invest more of my time educating myself on the space than I do my money. I spend a couple of hours every week broadening my knowledge by speaking with friends, listening to podcasts, reading books and learning from an online course in digital. Like Amundsen, I've gone and found my Inuit experts in this space, and I am participating in what I learn and understand.

3. Ride the crypto rollercoaster through to the end

Crypto assets are incredibly volatile and, like all investments, can feel like a rollercoaster. The crypto rollercoaster is one hell of a ride, having made investors eye-watering amounts of money some years as well as giving them their share of extreme downturns in others. The crypto rollercoaster is like watching all equity markets in fast-forward, sharing the same behavioural biases, big swings, sharp turns and sudden drops that we've seen over the years, all happening at ten times the speed.

4. Invest what you can afford to lose

To ensure my safety belt is securely fastened for the ride ahead, when it comes to crypto, I only invest what I can afford to lose from my tomorrow fund, which is about 3–5%. Why 3–5%? Because personally I feel I can afford to lose about 5% of my investments without seriously compromising my future financial freedom, and because crypto assets make up between 3–5% (3.9%, August 2022) of the total value of world stock markets (Coin98, 2022). Therefore, while I am a little exposed, I've diversified my investments and am only risking as much as I feel comfortable with.

I'm also investing on a regular basis, making steps towards a long-term goal (decades, not days). I'm diversifying my investments across numerous crypto assets because I can't predict who the winners and losers will be in the future. I'm seeing the ride through to the end rather than jumping off the tracks when the crypto rollercoaster takes a sudden drop, or the Sirens cry out.

Because crypto markets are extremely volatile and still a relatively new space (Bitcoin was created in 2009), I'd recommend investing from your day-after-tomorrow fund. Your today battery must be fully charged. From crypto to shares, whatever the asset and whatever the sector, it's incredibly risky to invest everything you have, or worse, borrow money or use a credit card to invest, especially in the hope of getting rich quick.

No matter what the Sirens are calling, borrowing to speculate – putting your today battery at risk – is more likely to see you washed up on the rocks. Amundsen succeeded in his expedition to the South Pole because he set off with plenty of supplies (food, water, medical equipment) and a contingency plan in place. His today battery was fully charged. Be like Amundsen and have a rainy-day fund and surplus savings just in case, so that you're neither borrowing to invest, nor investing what you can't afford to lose. This way, when markets are volatile, you can still weather the storm and not end up under an avalanche of debt.

5. Diversify your investment

When investing in crypto, aim to diversify across different currencies and digital assets. Again, this is a divisive topic in the crypto space, with Bitcoin maximalists believing that Bitcoin is the answer to everything, versus those who feel that the likes of Cardano, Ethereum or Solana have the most growth potential. The point is, don't invest your money in just one crypto asset. By diversifying your investments, you educate yourself on the whole crypto space and form your own opinion.

A final warning: Crypto transactions are taxable

As a decentralised form of digital 'money,' crypto can feel a little offgrid, but as a final warning for anyone considering investing in the space, please remember that crypto transactions and investments are taxable. If you are earning crypto assets that you might receive from either your employer as a form of non-cash payment, or if you are earning through mining, then you will be liable to paying income tax and capital gains tax. Remember that an awareness of your financial situation is the foundation to being able to make solid, long-term decisions, so don't get caught in a taxing situation by forgetting to state your investment earnings to HMRC. If you need more information about how taxes apply to crypto, you can visit the HMRC website.

Remember, it's so important to understand what you're investing in – this is only a basic guide. There are brilliant resources available that provide further education on this topic.

What makes crypto an asset

The digital asset space and the world of DeFi are still in the growing phase. There are now around 15,000 different cryptocurrencies in the world, of which around 60–100 are relatively well-known (Bitcoin, Cardano, Ethereum, Solana, etc). Their combined capital market value is circa $3 trillion, which is greater than the FTSE 100. There are also 400 different cryptocurrency exchanges where you can buy and sell digital money, and this will only continue to grow (Ossinger, 2021). Not only is the number of digital currencies out there increasing and growing in value, but brands, investors and users engaging with digital assets is evolving as well. The use of NFTs is evolving too through collaborations with offline brands, exclusive online clubs and even opportunities to co-purchase metaproperties. When it comes to the value of crypto, you need to look at its cash flow, scarcity value and utility. These three properties make it an asset.

Cash flow

When you invest in shares in the likes of Apple, Disney, Nike or Microsoft, you are buying into a share of those businesses and their capability to create cashflow. As they sell more products, they make more revenue, and if they make a profit, it can be paid to you as dividends or re-invested in the business to help it grow faster. This is how you make money. The same principle is true for a start-up, but these are inherently riskier because you are buying into the hope that they will be successful in the future, and as such, generate cash flow in the long term. Many startups have negative cashflow for several years. It took Tesla eighteen years to report its first full annual profit (Boudette, 2021). This illustrates the importance of thinking in decades not days. Many people use property to create cash flow, either by renting their home on Airbnb, or by having a second property to rent out.

Does crypto have cashflow? Yes and no. While owning cryptocurrency doesn't create cash flow, or pay you dividends like stocks, if you participate in DeFi on a 'Proof of Work' (PoW) network, you can become a 'miner' and strike digital gold ('payment' in the form of the network's native token, like a Bitcoin) by using computer power to verify transactions for cryptocurrencies. In a 'Proof of Stake' (PoS) network, you get 'paid' interest for staking your asset, for example, Cardano, or you can 'stake' and get paid in interest.

Scarcity value

Bitcoin also uses scarcity. Only 21 million Bitcoins will ever exist. It was designed to be scarce so the number of Bitcoins that you can 'mine' halves over time, which will ultimately drive up the price, because unlike tangible, centralised money, Bitcoins can't be reprinted.

Another investment route you might go down is to invest in scarce or 'rare' assets, like Chanel handbags or Rolex watches. These assets have utility (as you can wear them), but there are people who invest in these products for the purposes of re-selling them at a higher price because their value increases over time. In fact, over the last ten years, Rolexes have outperformed many asset classes, including gold, property and the stock market. To create scarcity, Rolex and Chanel manage supply and invest heavily in their brands so that they remain desirable to own.

Scarcity is also a feature of NFTs. A great example of this is the Bored Ape Yacht Club (BAYC). It is the rock 'n roll of NFT collections, having graced the cover of *Rolling Stone* magazine in November 2021. There are only 10,000 NFT ape avatars available, and investors in the club include Eminem, Jimmy Fallon, Steph Curry, Snoop Dogg and Shaquille O'Neal. The BAYC collection is not only highly desirable due to its finite supply (and, therefore, its scarcity), but because it is so much more than a JPEG of an ape avatar. BAYC is also an immersive fantastical world, an exclusive online social club, and a cult brand, which exists off-chain and in real life. An Adidas collaboration launched at the end of 2021 signified BAYC's influence: it has pulled fashion design into the metaverse and arguably acquired a similar status and cultural weight as the likes of Chanel in the process. Owning an NFT like BAYC is what drives up its scarcity value. We're seeing more and more NFTs trading on scarcity, but also offering utility, because they can be used to give you access to exclusive clubs.

Utility

A utility is something you buy to use. A car to drive, a handbag to wear, a house to live in and a watch to tell the time. Utilities, like a house, tend to be a sound investment because when you rent them out, they create cash flow. In some cases, a property can also benefit from scarcity. A villa on the coast of the South of France, like St Tropez, is a scarce utility (it is limited and desirable) so it's in high demand, which increases its value.

Does crypto have utility? Yes and no. Bitcoin, the original digital money, was designed for use as a medium of exchange, a store of value and a unit of account. Because Bitcoin has been so volatile and has grown in value exponentially in the past thirteen years, its utility has changed. Satoshi invented the currency in 2009 to solve the problem of making digital money, and it was originally used to exchange money or send a remittance abroad without heavy exchange fees. It went on to become so appreciated that its value soared – coining a new nickname for itself: 'digital gold'. Investors in this space are unlikely to 'spend' cryptocurrency – it is more like a scarce asset. You may know the story of Laszlo Hanyecz. He purchased two pizzas with 10,000 Bitcoins (BTC) in 2010. By May 2021, 10,000 BTC was equivalent to around 365 million dollars. How would you feel today knowing you'd spent hundreds of millions of dollars on a pizza? Especially if you were reminded of that fact every year on 22 May, officially dubbed #BitcoinPizzaDay. . . (Sparks, 2022).

While some of these cryptocurrencies have utility value, for example Ethereum, which allows users to create smart contracts to transact with each other without a trusted central authority; others don't have a utility value, which is why it's essential to keep educating yourself on this space and keep a balanced, long-term view as to how crypto will evolve. Flip the crypto coin, and it remains a gamble as to which of the two sides will come up tops. No one could have predicted its exponential growth back in 2010 when Bitcoin was being used to buy pizza, and it's likely that we can't even begin to imagine what the future of

DeFi, and digital assets will look like in another thirteen years – whatever side the coin lands.

To help mitigate the volatility in the crypto space, 'stablecoins' were invented. These are cryptocurrencies that peg their value to conventional (fiat) money, for example the US dollar. Stablecoins, as the name suggests, are supposed to provide stability in comparison to other crypto assets, and protect investors from volatile crypto prices. This offers greater utility because in theory you could convert $100 into a stablecoin that can be sent anywhere in the world and used to buy local fiat currency. This is a good example of how crypto and decentralised finance are directly competing with traditional banks.

One example is El Salvador, where the use of Bitcoin and its infrastructure to send remittances from abroad has been validated. In 2020, nearly 70% of the Salvadoran population received remittance payments totalling nearly $6 billion. Its president, Nayib Bukele, estimates that money services providers like Western Union and MoneyGram will lose $400 million a year in commissions for remittances thanks to the country's Bitcoin adoption (Sigalos, 2021). Longer term, another benefit is education of its population. Assuming crypto continues to expand worldwide, then Salvadorans will benefit from their understanding of Bitcoin, crypto and DeFi more broadly (Morris, 2022).

However, in May 2022, stablecoins Terra and Luna collapsed, sending tokens tumbling from a high of $118 (£96) to $0.09 (Tidy, 2022), resulting in Terraform Labs, the company behind TerraUSD and Terra Luna taking the unprecedented step of halting trading on its blockchain. This crash has resulted in a number of countries calling for stablecoins to be regulated, with the UK Treasury laying out plans in April 2022 to do so, meaning they could become a 'widespread means of payment', bridging a gap between fiat and DeFi.

***

The new kids on the blockchain are here to stay, and there is no doubt that crypto is one of the most exciting and innovative areas of finance and technology. Some of the world's smartest people are leaving well-paid jobs in both finance and technology – places like Apple, Google and JP Morgan – to go and work in this space.

NFTs are becoming more sophisticated and interactive than we could have ever dreamed when digital money was first invented in 2009. The metaverse is expanding and DeFi presents all kinds of opportunities to empower the future of finance, where everyone can access, buy, sell and verify digital assets. Not only is the future of finance evolving in a way that we couldn't have imagined as recently as fifteen years ago, but technologies like the blockchain could also see the future evolve to one that is more privacy-driven. Unless you're Gen Z, many of us are accustomed to a world where companies and social media have amassed vast amounts of consumer data and used or passed it on in ways that many of us haven't consented to. Unfortunately, these privacy issues are yet to be resolved, and Web 3.0 and the blockchain present a potential solution.

While Web 2.0 has driven incredible technological progress in this world, Blockchain technology allows us to imagine a future where data belongs to individuals rather than being owned by one entity, serving as a secure and transparent algorithm that will allow transactions and contracts to exist. The metaverse is still nascent, and we need both the hardware and software to envisage the world that Mark Zuckerberg sees. At the time of writing, Augmented Reality and Virtual Reality have proved popular in gaming and the world of learning & development. In 2022, the wealth manager I worked for created an avatar of me giving presentations on investing for new trainee financial advisors. Time will tell if we move more of our personal and professional lives onto the metaverse.

I recommend anyone curious about the crypto world dedicate more time to learning about it. Becoming aware is the most powerful way to educate yourself about this space.

16

Can Crypto Be
A Force For Good?

'Bitcoin and other cryptocurrencies have an energy
and environmental problem. But if done right, it
might be possible to channel all that energy into
something good for the planet.'
— *Forbes* (Rhodes, 2021)

You're now familiar with the idea of your money
being a force for good: you know what ESG
means, and how to invest your money to accelerate
the transition to a net-zero future. You're also now
familiar with cryptocurrency and digital assets. How
does crypto, and the energy required to mine it, fit
into responsible investing?

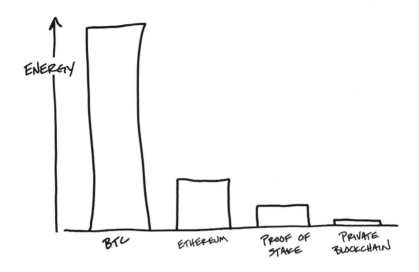

The impact of mining

As cryptocurrencies continue to rapidly evolve and grow in value, so does the incentive to become a 'miner'. Mining consumes considerable amounts of electrical power, and as mining grows, the amount of energy required to use blockchain technology rises along with it. The Cambridge Centre for Alternative Finance (The CCAF) estimates that Bitcoin accounts for 0.59% of the total global electricity production and consumption (CCAF, March 2022). Although some have argued that Bitcoin only uses half the energy used by the traditional global banking system, if it were a country, it would be among the top thirty energy consuming nations in the world. This raises questions around the impact that mining and the blockchain will have on energy consumption and the wellbeing of our planet, such as:

• Where is the electricity coming from?

• Is the energy renewable?

• What is being done to reduce the amount of non-renewable energy used to mine?

• What do we need to consider when it comes to investing responsibly in cryptocurrency, or becoming a miner?

Mining and blockchains are coming under greater scrutiny for their energy consumption. In May 2021, Tesla CEO Elon Musk announced that the company would suspend vehicle purchases using Bitcoin and only resume once mining shifts to more sustainable energy sources (BBC News, 2021). While taking a strong and public stance on the issue is a solid start, we know that boycotting or divesting rarely solves the problem as effectively as engaging people, businesses and brands to do better. What else can, and is, being done in the space so that we can mine, or invest in digital assets that mine, responsibly?

An important part of this debate is understanding the two different kinds of crypto verification (ie, the consensus mechanism). Proof of Work (PoW) and Proof of Stake (PoS) impact the environment differently. PoW is the original system and was used to mine the first cryptocurrency, Bitcoin. It makes up the majority of blockchains, including the original version of Ethereum. In a PoW system, crypto miners around the world race to solve difficult puzzles first, with the winner rewarded by being the one to update the blockchain, and in return, receive a certain amount of crypto. The way the PoW system works means that at any one time there will be millions of computers working towards the same problem, with many using specialised and energy-intensive Graphic Processing Units (GPUs) to mine. As there can only be one 'winner' from all the competing miners, PoW is a particularly inefficient process that results in a tremendous amount of energy waste.

PoS, on the other hand, is a much newer system that has become more popular in the last five years. PoS has become more prevalent with Ethereum, the world's second-largest cryptocurrency, switching to the PoS model, which has already slashed the blockchain's energy usage by 99% (Whitwam, 2022). With PoS, blockchains have a system of validators who stake their own crypto to earn a chance to validate new transactions, update the blockchain and earn a reward for their efforts. The network chooses a validator to update the blockchain according to how much crypto they've staked and how long they've had it staked for, rewarding people who invest the most for longest.

You can probably already see how this is a more energy-efficient method of blockchain verification, as it uses less energy. It's claimed PoS will cut Ethereum's energy consumption by as much as 99% (Beekhuizen, 2021). It's worth noting that PoS does require technical knowledge from validators, and being a validator is a riskier commitment than being a PoW miner, as PoS tends to involve having a portfolio of crypto that you're willing to stake to obtain more and runs the risks of losing some or all of your stake.

The PoW system (rather than PoS) is posing one of the biggest challenges in the crypto space, because the computer power required by 'miners' to verify transactions and confirm nodes on the network uses a huge amount of energy. There are two main actions we can take to address this issue:

1. Look at why so much electric power is needed, and where possible, reduce it.

2. Ensure that the energy being used by 'miners' is coming from a renewable source.

Remember, the number of Bitcoin left available is halving all the time – giving the asset scarcity. At the same time, computers are evolving and becoming more powerful, so can use less electricity for processes like mining. Despite this, one reason computers use so much energy to mine is because they heat up when using a lot of power, so a lot of electricity is used to cool them back down. To counteract this, we are seeing the rise of 'green miners' in countries like Iceland and Norway (places that are naturally cold). Energy isn't required to cool the servers back down as the air outside is chilly enough to do the trick. As well as this, almost 100% of Iceland's electricity is produced by renewable sources, and about 97% in Norway (Carroll, 2019). So, it's worth remembering that a digital coin being mined in the likes of Iceland and Norway using renewable energy has significantly less impact on the environment than those mined in China using coal-powered electricity. That said, mining was banned by the Chinese government in May 2021. What we've seen since is a huge shift in PoW mining all over the world. This 'mining boom' is happening in places like the US and Canada, with miners locating where it is cold and/or where they have access to renewable energy, either in the form of wind farms or hydro-electric power.

So, a bit like in the real world, we are seeing a transition in the mining world to net-zero, where miners are thinking about how to both reduce the energy consumption associated with mining and ensure that the energy being used is renewable. In fact, there are even those who would argue that mining for crypto is causing an increase in the demand for renewable energy.

What about other DeFi assets?

Initiatives like the WWF are taking bigger strides in making crypto a force for good. The WWF launched a set of NFTs to try and protect some of the most endangered animals on the planet. The WWF has partnered with some exciting artists all over the world to create Non-Fungible Art (NFA) avatars in the likes of the

Amur Tiger, Giant Panda and Mountain Gorilla, with a finite number of each asset created to represent the number of each species of animals left. WWF have leveraged the scarcity value of NFTs in a poignant way to show just how close to extinction these species are. Proceeds from investing in these NFAs are used for the protection of endangered animals. WWF have chosen to create their limited range of NFAs on the Polygon (PoS) network because of its low environmental impact.

WWF's initiative asks some important questions that are improving environmental awareness in the world of DeFi:

• How can we use this new technology to help address poverty and protect nature?

• Could the future of NFTs mean that we recognise the value that nature offers us, even going so far as to put a value on the Amazon rainforest to stop people cutting it down?

Crypto is still in its infancy but can play a role when it comes to using your money as a force for good if it is mined in the right way and put towards sustainable causes. If you're investing in, or mining, crypto, can it be done responsibly? And could the future even see DeFi evolve in a way that connects nature and the prosperity of the planet with our own prosperity? The future is exciting, but the future is also unknown, and it's essential to keep that in mind when it comes to earning it, keeping it and growing it.

PART FOUR
PRESERVE IT

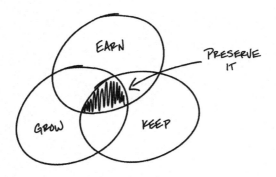

'Many people take no care of their money till they come nearly to the end of it, and others do just the same with their time.'
— Johann Wolfgang von Goethe

17

Alpine Descent

'Decumulation – the process of making your money last throughout your retirement – is the nastiest, hardest problem in finance.'
— William Sharpe, a Nobel Prize winner for his work on financial theory

What goes up, must come down. Throughout this book, we've covered how you can earn, keep and grow your money. I've explained why it's important to plan for your future, how to do it, the bumps in the road you need to account for, and the pitfalls to avoid. In fact, I hope now that you've reached this chapter, you're saving for a pension so your future self can retire comfortably – or know the steps you need to take to be able to do so.

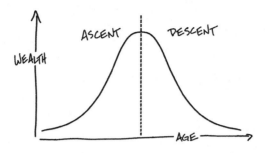

Once you've climbed the slow and steady path to financial freedom and your future self has reached retirement age, you'd be forgiven for thinking that your job is done. Now it's just a case of spending that nest egg, right? Well, not quite. In this chapter I'm going to talk about what happens when you want to withdraw the money you've saved into your day-after-tomorrow fund and enjoy a comfortable retirement.

With the 'new normal' being to live to a hundred, the average man will run out of money ten years before he dies, and the average woman will run out of money twelve and a half years before she dies. These are scary statistics, so it's vitally important that you plan carefully.

When you're *earning it, keeping it and growing it,* long-term inflation is a big risk to your future prosperity. When you're coming down the retirement mountain, you're exposed to the risk of inflation and the challenge of longevity (ie, how long you're going to live). Think about when you retire and how long after that you're going to live for. How is inflation going to impact your retirement plans? What is the cost of goods going to look like ten or twenty years after you retire? I know that a million pounds might seem like a lot of money now, but thirty years from now, that million pounds may only be worth £330,000 due to inflation. William Sharpe, a Nobel Prize winner for his work on financial theory, is said to have referred to 'decumulation' (the process of making your money last throughout your retirement) as the 'nastiest, hardest problem in finance.'

You need to invest your money, so that it grows and outpaces inflation. You also need to know the right time to take your money out, and how much you should withdraw, so you can preserve it for the whole of your retirement. Everything that worked in your favour on the way up, is working against you on the way down. Taking your money out is more fraught with difficulty than putting your money in. Here's how to map your route down 'retirement mountain' in five steps.

1. Map your route

For any hike, knowing where you want to get to, how you'll get there, how long it will take and what obstacles may be in the way is crucial. Your retirement is no different. Just having a pot of money is not enough. You need to plan carefully to make sure it lasts the rest of your life. Considering various scenarios and continuing to invest it wisely is key so that your 'pot' continues to grow, and you can live comfortably until your final days. Preparing for the worst-case scenario means not running out of money in retirement, and having some money left over.

2. Go with a guide

Unless you're an experienced hiker, climbing a mountain with someone else – who has either done the journey before or who is a guide – is a better idea than going it alone. Find an Inuit. It's important that you learn how to manage your financial journey in the same way that Amundsen did in the race to the South Pole. If you've got a company pension and you've suddenly retired and discovered that you have a lot of money, then you really need to get some guidance to help you understand how long you might live for, what might happen to inflation and how much you can afford to take out of your pension pot each year.

You need to plan to come down the mountain in the same way you plan to climb up it. A financial advisor can help you understand how to manage your money now and advise you what your retirement will look like. A financial advisor will also help you to review, plan and adjust to your changing financial situation. I absolutely advise you to seek out expert help now to ensure you live prosperously after you retire.

3. Shield yourself from the 'wind chill'

When you retire, you're no longer earning any money. This means you're no longer topping up your savings and risk running out of money. It's like coming off the mountain and experiencing the 'wind chill'. How sensitive you are to 'wind chill' will depend on how you invest your money, but crucially, on how and when you take it out. The more you take out, the higher the risk. Everyone will need different amounts of money when they retire, so the only way to make sure that you're making the right decisions for your personal circumstances is to seek help from an expert.

Remember how we discussed the volatility of markets? If you've got a million pounds saved in your pension and you want to take out £40,000 a year to live off, you'll obviously end up with less money in your pension. You'll only have £960,000 left of those one million pounds. If the market then falls by another 10% (which is likely to happen) and then you take out another £40,000, then when the market recovers (which it will eventually do), you'll have less money to grow. When the market recovers it will be recovering on a smaller amount. Because you've taken money out, you don't benefit, which is the exact opposite of what happens when you're investing your money before you retire. Can you see why I say that coming down the mountain is more difficult than climbing the mountain?

When you're young and saving for retirement, the highs and lows of the investment rollercoaster are actually less scary than when you hit retirement, because when and how you get your returns by sixty-five doesn't really matter: So long as you hit your target, who cares if your money grew steadily each year or if you just had a fantastic final few years (although this can be emotionally taxing, even for the savviest investor)? Just like the weather, investment markets cannot be controlled, but you can prepare for when the weather changes. In a financial sense, this is investing into the right portfolio: a combination of funds that have been designed to mitigate these risks.

4. Pace yourself

You have your guide; you've developed your route and how long you think you'll be hiking for (your financial plan and life expectancy estimation). You're kitted up and prepared and you've invested to protect against that nastiest problem in finance – inflation, coupled with longevity. Now you need to work out how quickly to descend the other side of the mountain safely (ie, how much to spend and when).

You need to plan your investments around how you're going to spend that money over the next ten, twenty and thirty-plus years. How can you spend your money confidently without running out of money? Can you afford to spend 4–6% of your savings a year? Or can you only afford to spend

2–4% of your savings a year? Having enough cash to live on in your retirement is important, but how do you know how much is enough? This is where your guide can help you. One of the things that a lot of people do as soon as they retire is draw down on their pension. They see a big pot of money and they forget that they may live for another twenty or thirty-plus years, so they enjoy spending their money on holidays, house extensions, new cars and new homes, without realising the consequences that follow. It may be that you can afford to do this, but it may be that you can't. If you make a mistake and spend your retirement pot too quickly, you could find yourself in serious difficulty in your later years. Therefore, we need to be cautious once we've reached the summit of our earnings and start descending into our savings, during retirement.

Getting financial advice can be a great way to help you make some good decisions about your long-term financial prosperity. It can also reduce stress in your relationship with your partner if you see a financial advisor together. Going through your finances jointly actually gives you both a kind of open window which will take some of that financial stress away.

Regularly checking in on your financial plan is important so that you become more dynamic with your spending. In hiking terms, for an hour or two, the weather gods may have been smiling down on you and so you're able to see ahead and walk quicker without too much worry, but an hour or so later, the skies may darken, visibility is impaired, and you need to slow down to avoid making a wrong step. In the same way, for some years the markets may be good to you. You may decide that it's OK to spend a little more than usual this year, so you treat yourself and your family. Some years you may need to pare back and spend less to level out your plan and make sure you'll continue to have the right amount of money to invest and generate an income for you.

Because you're not earning money in retirement, you don't want to live out those years in 'battery saving mode', so it's essential that (where possible) you don't withdraw large sums when the stock market crashes, that you stay invested (remember decades, not days), and where necessary, you seek help from your guide.

5. Leave your path the way you'd wish to find it

Finally, being an environmentally responsible hiker is a must. We all have a responsibility to look after the planet, and in the same way that littering on your way up or down a mountain is a no-no, we want to leave these walks and trails in pristine condition for future generations to enjoy, just as we have.

18

How To Leave
A Financial Legacy

'Tell me and I forget, teach me and I may remember,
involve me and I learn.'
— Benjamin Franklin

It's time to graduate from the 'Earn It, Keep It,
Grow It School of Financial Education'. We've
covered everything on the financial spectrum: the
steps you can take to get out of debt, how to build
up an emergency cash buffer, calculating your net
worth, planning for your retirement, and using
your money as a force for good. We've looked at
how your investments can help the world transition to net-zero, and how crypto can be part of your
financial freedom.

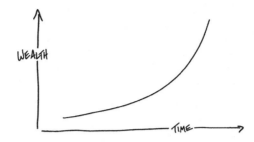

At the start of this book, we looked at the importance of being able to talk about money. In this final chapter I'd like to share the importance of getting into the habit of also having those conversations with your children, or the future generations around you. I hope that you will continue to invest time in furthering your own financial education. It's essential that you also go one step further and break the cycle of debt and financial insecurity for future generations to come by imparting what you've learned. It's our responsibility to empower the next generation to be even better when it comes to money – better savers, better decision-makers, better financial planners, better and more confident investors and, crucially, better ancestors to the planet and the people living on it.

Conversations worth having

Financial education from a young age is something I place a lot of value on. When my children were born, I wrote a children's book called *Save Your Acorns*, a story that teaches children about the importance of saving and investing money, and the consequences of wasting it, in a way that is fun and easy to understand (Gardner, 2016). I also created a fun card game called 'Silly Monkeys' based on the characters in the book. My aim with *Save Your Acorns* and 'Silly Monkeys' was to help children get to grips with the basics of money, encourage good saving habits, and to open a dialogue between parents and their children.

If you have, or want to have, children, it's important that you start having conversations with them early on in their lives to give them a head-start with savvy saving habits. It's vital that children understand the basics of budgeting and saving, and it shouldn't be just one conversation at the dinner table – it needs to be ongoing. It's never too early to gently introduce children to the concept of money. Using money in role play is highly effective for toddlers and pre-schoolers. As children get a little older and start developing a deeper understanding of numbers, it's important to start showing them good money management. You can also introduce the idea of 'needs' and 'wants', and delayed gratification. This will put them in good stead for their rainy-day, tomorrow and day-after-tomorrow savings pots, as well as helping them to understand how to manage and keep money when they start earning.

A few years ago, a financial literacy programme was introduced in Wales called 'Talk, Learn, Do' (Money & Pensions Service, 2016). Primary school children and their parents joined a course that encouraged parents to talk to their children about money and give their children a go at managing it. If, like me, you've ever been held hostage by your children at the supermarket checkout because they're screaming that they want sweets and you end up caving in because you're embarrassed, then you'll appreciate how valuable this intervention was for the parents who participated.

The interesting thing about this programme was that some parents also benefited. Some had managed to pay down some of their debt and improve how they were managing their household finances (IFF, 2018). What this proves to me is that being open about money and talking about it with friends and family is a good thing. It shouldn't be taboo. How money works and how you can use it to protect yourself and your family really matters. When the conversations are brought out into the open, everyone benefits and so I hope that, at the least, my book starts a conversation.

How to make your child a millionaire in retirement

I hope you also benefit from this book by learning that you could make your child a millionaire in retirement. Let me get one thing straight: you do not need to be a millionaire, or even a high earner, to make your child a millionaire. I'll show you how.

Do you remember my friend, Jess? Well, I'm delighted to tell you that she's had a baby. Like every parent, she wants her baby's future to be secure, but as I've said before, we're all living longer, and babies born today are expected to live to see a hundred. This means that it can be difficult to know what to do to ensure your child's long-term financial future.

One way of securing your child's future is to open a pension for them as soon as they're born, which we touched on where we covered tax wrappers. Most people don't realise you can open a pension for a child, but you can, and you should, consider doing this. You can set up a pension for your baby in the week that he or she is born and contribute £5 a day to your baby's pension fund until your child is ten years old. You can then stop investing completely and leave the money where it is. Through investment, the tax incentive of 25% that the government gives you for every pound that you save in a pension (wrapper), and the magic of compound interest, this will grow to over one million pounds by the time your child turns sixty-five.

Isn't that a cool thing to do for your kid? It's something that Jess, Emily and Paul have all done for their children, and I hope you will consider it too. And as a reminder, if you invest sustainably, this is twenty-seven times more impactful for the planet than eating less red meat, flying less or cycling to work, meaning you're securing their financial futures in a world worth living in.

Family fortunes

When we're all financially resilient, and teaching our children to be the same, we'll hopefully be living in a world where money is not a major cause of stress. When you're not worried about losing your job, when you're not worrying about bills, and when you're protected against living a hundred-year life and the inflation that goes along with it, then your mental health will be better, your family will be happier, and you'll be confident in making the choices you want for your financial freedom.

A big theme of this book is to 'earn it, keep it, grow it' in a consistent way. Healthy habits have a compounding effect, helping you to have awareness, act and accelerate your plans. It goes without saying that the earlier you start compounding, the better, and that includes introducing the concept as early as possible. We need to be having daily conversations about money, and the risk and reward that comes with investing, with our children. If we can teach them how to earn money, keep it and grow their wealth through the wonder of compound interest, we will give them the best chance of achieving financial freedom.

The final piece of compounding is what happens when we, as parents or grandparents, teach our children the simple message of 'earn it, keep it, grow it'. If we teach them how money works, we'll equip them with the skills to build financial resilience in their own lives. It is our responsibility to break the cycle of money having a negative impact on our mental health, relationships and the planet, so that together we are empowered to enjoy financial wellbeing in a world worth living in.

As part of this book's financial legacy, all proceeds will go to RedSTART, the financial education charity that I co-founded. This means that just by purchasing a copy for yourself, you have already contributed to the financial future and education of UK primary schools and their pupils who need it the most. (To learn more about RedSTART and how they are trying to change the game for every primary school child in the UK by 2030, head to the charity's website at https://redstarteducate.org.)

A Final Word From The Author

'Habits are the compound interest of self-improvement.'
— James Clear, *Atomic Habits*

Thank you for reading this book. I hope you have enjoyed it and feel empowered on your path to financial freedom. The next steps are all about taking action, and if you can remember to be like Amundsen, Joseph and Ulysses, and form sustainable lifelong habits, you should be able to weather the storms and the bumps in the road.

I'd love to hear how you get on, so do reach out any time. You can find me @robertjgardner on Instagram and Twitter, and on LinkedIn at https://uk.linkedin.com/in/robertjgardner and don't forget to revisit the

Financial Freedom scorecard at https://yourfinancialfreedom.scoreapp.com to review your financial situation.

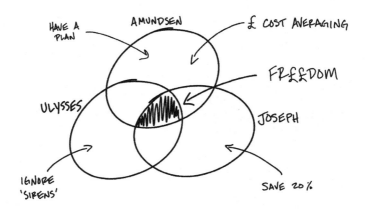

Remember: earn it, keep it and grow it are the three money habits to help you achieve financial freedom in a world worth living in.

Good luck!

Robert

A Visual Reminder Of
The Key Concepts In The
Book By Carl Richards

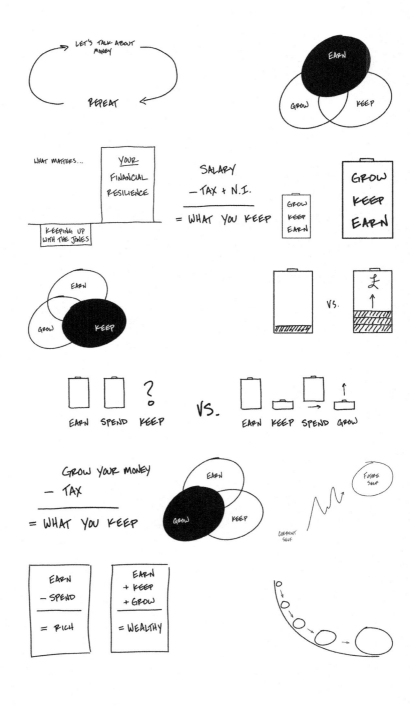

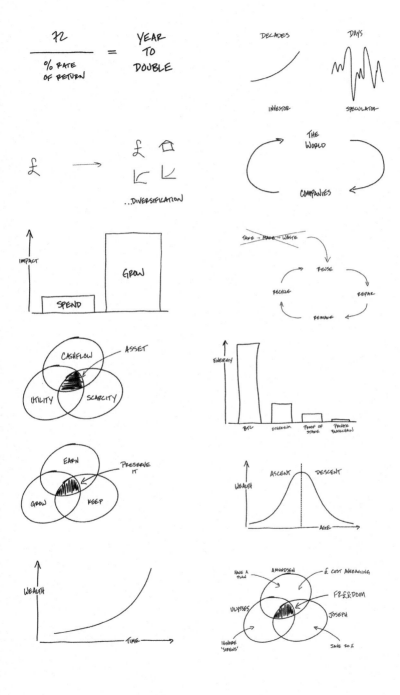

Further Reading

Becoming debt-free

Money Helper – Paying off your credit card. Credit card debt can quickly mount up if you don't pay your card off in full each month. Here's how to stop that happening: www.moneyhelper.org.uk/en/everyday-money/types-of-credit/paying-off-your-credit-card

Step Change Debt Charity. Get free help from the UK's leading debt charity. Their online advice tool has helped over 1.7 m people. You can create a budget and get a personal action plan with practical next steps: www.stepchange.org

Debt Advice Foundation is a national debt advice and education charity offering free, confidential support and advice to anyone worried about debt. Their Personal Debt Analyser is a free, easy to use debt assessment tool that will help you to understand the full extent of your debt problem as well as provide practical advice on what to do next: www.debtadvice-foundation.org/debt-tools/debt-analyser/

National Debtline offers free debt advice online through its digital advice tool and its web guides, fact sheets and sample letters: www.nationaldebtline.org

Managing your money and taxes

Remember to update your tax code if you start a new job: www.gov.uk/tax-codes/how-to-update-your-tax-code

If you do not already have a National Insurance number, you only need to apply for one if you're planning to start work: www.gov.uk/apply-national-insurance-number

Use the Bank of England inflation calculator to check how prices in the UK have changed over time, from 1209 to 2019: www.bankofengland.co.uk/monetary-policy/inflation/inflation-calculator

Pension and retirement

Do you know how long you'll live? Enter your age and sex in our calculator to find out your life expectancy: www.ons.gov.uk/peoplepopulationandcommunity/ healthandsocialcare/healthandlifeexpectancies/ articles/lifeexpectancycalculator/2019-06-07

Workplace pensions – contribution matching: www. gov.uk/workplace-pensions

Money Helper – contribution matching: www.mon-eyhelper.org.uk/en/pensions-and-retirement/ building-your-retirement-pot/contribution-matching

Defined contribution – AVCs and FSAVCs: Money Helper www.moneyhelper.org.uk/en/pensions-and-retirement/building-your-retirement-pot/what-are-avcs-and-fsavcs

PLSA – Retirement Savings Standards: www.retire-mentlivingstandards.org.uk

Gov.uk – The new State Pension – What you'll get: www.gov.uk/new-state-pension/what-youll-get

References

Chapter 1: Let's talk about money

Department for Work and Pensions, 'Over ten million people to live to 100', Gov.UK (30 December 2010), www.gov.uk/government/news/over-ten-million-people-to-live-to-100, accessed 17 June 2022

Dunn, G, 'Why we'd rather talk about sex than money – and how I plan to change it', *The Guardian* (2 November 2016), www.theguardian.com/money/2016/nov/02/bad-with-money-talking-about-finances-gaby-dunn-podcast, accessed 17 June 2022

Franklin, B, 'The Way To Wealth', preface to *Poor Richard's Almanack* (1758)

Green, N, 'One in three Brits don't know how much pension to save', Unbiased.com (3 December 2020), www.unbiased.co.uk/news/financial-adviser/ one-in-three-brits-don-t-know-how-much-pension-to-save, accessed 17 June 2022

Hughes, A, 'Britons find money harder to talk about than mental health', *The Independent* (30 April 2019), www.independent.co.uk/life-style/money-mental-health-social-norms-poll-a8893021.html, accessed 17 June 2022

McCoy, M, et al, 'Exploring how one's primary financial conversant varies by marital status', *Journal of Financial Therapy* (2019), https://newprairiepress. org/cgi/viewcontent.cgi?article=1193&context=jft, accessed 17 June 2022

Roberts, A, 'Sex and finance are better for married people', CNN (14 February 2018), https://edition. cnn.com/2018/02/14/health/valentines-day-single-married-comparison-trnd/index.html, accessed 17 June 2022

Part One: Earn It

Kiyosaki, R, *Rich Dad Poor Dad*, Warner Books (1997)

Chapter 2: It's not what you earn, it's what you do with it that counts

Brigden, S, 'Interest rates: compound interest, AER and APR explained', MoneySavingExpert (6 April 2021), www.moneysavingexpert.com/banking/interest-rates, accessed 17 June 2022

Burton, T, 'SHMEE150 – Living the supercar dream', YouTube (no date), www.youtube.com/c/Shmee150/featured, accessed 22 June 2022

Clear, J *Atomic Habits*, Penguin Random House (2021)

Elkins, K, 'Shaq once blew through $1 million in under an hour, but now he saves 75% of his income', CNBC Make It (July 2019), www.cnbc.com/2019/07/16/shaq-saves-and-invests-75percent-of-his-income.html, accessed 17 June 2022

'#1931 Michael Jordan', *Forbes* (March 2022), www.forbes.com/profile/michael-jordan/?sh=461dec3b2d83, accessed 17 June 2022

Housel, M, *The Psychology of Money: Timeless lessons on wealth, greed and happiness*, Harriman House (2020)

'Shaquille O'Neal discusses investing, franchising, and donuts', The Investor Show [podcast], (November 2019), https://open.spotify.com/episode/6lm70DvAzbL0BOzwR0ZPTO, accessed 17 June 2022

Klarna, Terms and Conditions, Clause 3.1 'Standard Rate', Klarna https://cdn.klarna.com/1.0/shared/content/legal/terms/0/en_gb/account_agreement, accessed 17 June 2022

Lere, J, 'Say "No" to racing Mr and Mrs Jones', The Money Panel (28 October 2020), https://themoneypanel.co.uk/mr-and-mrs-jones, accessed 17 June 2022

Nichol, J, 'What is the net worth of NBA legend Dennis Rodman?' HITC (15 January 2022), www.hitc.com/en-gb/2022/01/15/dennis-rodman-net-worth, accessed 17 June 2022

ONS, 'Employee earnings in the UK: 2021', Gov.UK, (26 October 2021), www.ons.gov.uk/employmentandlabourmarket/peopleinwork/earningsandworkinghours/bulletins/annualsurveyofhoursandearnings/2021, accessed 17 June 2022

ONS, 'Consumer price inflation, annual rate 00: all items 2015 = 100', Gov.UK, (no date), www.ons.gov.uk/economy/inflationandpriceindices/timeseries/d7g7/mm23, accessed 17 June 2022

Oprah Winfrey Network, 'The time Shaquille O'Neal spent $1 million in one day', Oprah's Master Class [podcast] (September 2017), https://oprahs-master-class-the-podcast.simplecast.com/episodes/shaquille-oneal-7_KzwOX7, accessed 17 June 2022

Pou, P, 'Argentina's structural reforms of the 1990s', *Finance & Development: Quarterly Magazine of the IMF,* March 2000, 37:1

Ross, C, 'Since the Covid-19 pandemic, BNPL schemes have increased in popularity, with one in three people having used retail finance for their purchases, spending on average around £560 per year', Fablicious (10 September 2020), https://fablious.co.uk/blog/how-lockdown-has-affected-bnpl, accessed 17 June 2022

Torre, PS, 'How (and why) athletes go broke', Vault (March 2009), https://vault.si.com/vault/2009/03/23/how-and-why-athletes-go-broke, accessed 17 June 2022

'Shmee150's net worth built on his love of exotic cars', Wealthy Genius (no date), www.wealthygenius.com/shmee150-net-worth, accessed 17 June 2022

White, A, 'Shaquille O'Neal recommends you save money from every paycheck, no matter how much', Select (January 2022), www.cnbc.com/select/shaquille-oneal-money-saving-advice, accessed 17 June 2022

Chapter 3: Understanding your payslip

Angeloni, C, 'Pensions tax relief mystifies Brits', *International Adviser* (May 2021), https://international-adviser.com/pensions-tax-relief-mystifies-brits, accessed 17 June 2022

Chapter 4: Become More Valuable: How to increase your earning potential

Hoffman, R, 'Success is about breakout opportunities', The Startup of You [podcast] (August 2022), https://open.spotify.com/episode/2grrJtdG dY8s1uiUcOennY?si=D6kMLfxoRjW_X1t3gQgCZQ, accessed 14 May 2023

Hoffman, R and Casnocha, B, *The Start-Up of You: Adapt to the future, invest in yourself, and transform your career*, Random House Business (2013)

Jordan, M, quoted in Goldman, R, and Papson, S, *Nike Culture: The Sign of the Swoosh*, Sage Publications (1998)

Kolb, DM and Williams, AC, 'Don't ask for a raise – negotiate it', *Harvard Business Review* (2 December 2021), https://hbr.org/2021/12/dont-ask-for-a-raise-negotiate-it, accessed 14 May 2023

LBC, 'University graduates "earn £3,000 more each year" than than those without a degree', LBC (29 February 2020), www.lbc.co.uk/news/uk/university-graduates-earn-3-000-more-each-year-tha, accessed 14 May 2023

Lopata, A, *Connected Leadership: How professional relationships underpin executive success*, Panoma Press (2020)

Loudenback, T and Gould, S, 'The first big career choice you make can haunt you for years - and cost you $1 million', Business Insider (22 September 2017), www.businessinsider.com/how-to-negotiate-salary-earn-more-2017-9, accessed 16 May 2023

Priestley, D, *Become a Key Person of Influence: The 5 step sequence to becoming one of the most highly valued and highly paid people in your industry*, Ecademy Press (2011)

Part Two: Keep It

Chakrabarty, A, 'Financial mistakes: Top 5 spending mistakes that may affect your savings', Financial Express (11 May 2022), www.financialexpress.com/money/financial-mistakes-top-5-spending-mistakes-that-may-curtail-your-savings/2521145, accessed 17 February 2023

Chapter 5: Building financial resilience

Clear, J, *Atomic Habits: An Easy and Proven Way to Build Good Habits and Break Bad Ones*, Penguin Random House (2021)

Franklin, B, 'The Way To Wealth', preface to *Poor Richard's Almanack* (1758)

Lawther, R, '51% of UK adults do not have enough emergency savings', International Adviser (19 July 2021), https://international-adviser.com/51-of-uk-adults-do-not-have-enough-emergency-savings, accessed 17 June 2022

'Debt and mental health', National Debt Line (no date), https://nationaldebtline.org/fact-sheet-library/debt-and-mental-health-ew, accessed 17 June 2022

Scott, E, 'Budgeting and mental health among skills we wish we'd learned at school', *Metro News* (September 2019), https://metro.co.uk/2019/09/13/budgeting-mental-health-among-skills-wish-wed-learned-school-10734293, accessed 17 June 2022

Chapter 6: Weatherproofing your finances

Clason, G, *The Richest Man in Babylon* (1926)

The Bible (King James Version), William Collins (2016)

Chapter 7: Why tax wrappers matter

UK House Price Index: July 2022, 'The average house deposit price in the UK is £292,000', ONS (no date), www.ons.gov.uk/economy/inflationandpriceindices/bulletins/housepriceindex/july2022, accessed 17 June 2022

Part Three: Grow It

Chapter 8: Meet your future self

'The new state pension – what you'll get', Gov.UK (no date), www.gov.uk/new-state-pension/what-youll-get, accessed 17 June 2022

Green, N, 'One in three Brits don't know how much pension to save', Unbiased.com (3 December 2020), www.unbiased.co.uk/news/financial-adviser/one-in-three-brits-don-t-know-how-much-pension-to-save, accessed 17 June 2022

Housel, M, *The Psychology of Money: Timeless lessons on wealth, greed and happiness*, Harriman House (2020)

Neilan, C, 'Bye-bye Bogof? Supermarket deals days' numbered as new research finds consumers spend £1,300 a year more when they take up buy-one, get-one-free offers', City A.M. (February 2016), www.cityam.com/bye-bye-bogof-deals-days-numbered-as-new-research-finds-consumers-spend-1300-a-year-more-when-they-take-up-buy-one-get-one-free-offers, accessed 17 June 2022

'Retirement Living Standards', Pensions and Lifetime Savings Association (no date), www.retirementlivingstandards.org.uk, accessed 17 June 2022

Royal London, 'Financial advice provides
£47,000 wealth uplift in a decade', Royal
London (28 November 2019), www.royallondon.
com / media / press-releases / 2019 / november /
financial-advice-provides-47000-wealth-uplift-
in-a-decade-new-research-from-royal-london-
and-the- international-longevity-centre, accessed
17 June 2022

Chapter 9: Calculate your net worth

Maunder, S, 'Buying a house or flat in London,'
Which? (February 2022) www.which.co.uk / money /
mortgages-and-property / first-time-buyers /
buying-a-home / buying-a-house-or-flat-in-london-
aJLfe3p12JiA, accessed September 2022

'Housing affordability in England and
Wales: 2019,' ONS (2019), www.ons.gov.uk /
peoplepopulationandcommunity / housing / bulletins /
housingaffordabilityinenglandandwales / 2019,
accessed September 2022

Partington, R, 'Home ownership among young
adults has "collapsed", study finds,' *The Guardian*
(16 February 2018), https: / / www.theguardian.com /
money / 2018 / feb / 16 / homeownership-among-
young-adults-collapsed-institute-fiscal-studies,
accessed September 2022

Ravikant, N, 'Seek wealth, not money or status. Wealth is having assets that earn while you sleep…' [tweet], Twitter (31 May 2018), https://twitter.com/naval/status/1002103497725173760?lang=en, accessed 17 February 2023

Westwater, H, 'Half of young people don't think they will be able to retire comfortably,' *The Big Issue* (12 January 2022), www.bigissue.com/news/social-justice/half-of-young-people-dont-believe-theyll-ever-be-able-to-retire-comfortably-cost-of-living, accessed 17 February 2023

Chapter 10: Compounding matters – get interested

Housel, M, 'Here's the most overlooked fact about how Warren Buffett amassed his fortune, says money expert,' CNBC (8 September 2020), www.cnbc.com/2020/09/08/billionaire-warren-buffett-most-overlooked-fact-about-how-he-got-so-rich.html, accessed 29 January 2023

Sather, A, '10 reasons why compounding interest is the 8th wonder of the world', eInvesting for Beginners (27 May 2021), https://einvesting for beginners.com/compounding-interest, accessed 29 January 2023

Chapter 11: In it to win it

Berger, R, 'Top 100 money quotes of all time', Forbes.com (30 April 2014), www.forbes.com/sites/robertberger/2014/04/30/top-100-money-quotes-of-all-time/?sh=1c279a834998, accessed 29 January 2023

Charts and data from MSCI's flagship global equity index, MSCI ACWI, www.msci.com/our-solutions/indexes/acwi, accessed 29 January 2023

Chapter 12: Diversify

Attenborough, D, '"Not fear, but hope" – Attenborough speech in full', BBC.co.uk (1 November 2021), www.bbc.co.uk/news/av/science-environment-59121615, accessed 29 January 2023

'Risks of CFD trading', CMC Markets (no date), www.cmcmarkets.com/en/learn-cfd-trading/risks-of-cfds, accessed 29 January 2023

Collins, J, *Great By Choice*, HarperBusiness (2001)

'Market cap for Apple Inc.', Finbox (no date), https://finbox.com/NASDAQGS:aapl/explorer/marketcap, accessed on 17 June 2022

Glaeser, E, Di Tella, R, Llach, L, 'Introduction to Argentine exceptionalism', Harvard Business School (27 October 2017), www.hbs.edu/faculty/Pages/download.aspx?name=LAER+Introduction+to+Argentine+Exceptionalism.pdf, accessed 29 January 2023

Sainato, M, '"We were sold off": WeWork's support staff face uncertain future as company collapses,' *The Guardian* (22 November 2019), www.theguardian.com/business/2019/nov/22/we-were-sold-off-weworks-support-staff-face-uncertain-future-as-company-collapses, accessed 29 January 2023

Robinson, J, 'Amundsen & the Inuits', Amundsen Sports (no date), https://amundsensports.com/amundsen-the-inuits, accessed September 2022

'Roald Amundsen North-West expedition 1903–06', Royal Museums Greenwich (no date), www.rmg.co.uk/stories/topics/roald-amundsen-north-west-passage-expedition-1903-06, accessed 29 January 2023

'Distribution of countries with largest stock markets worldwide as of January 2021, by share of total world equity market value', Statista Research Department (no date), www.statista.com/statistics/710680/global-stock-markets-by-country, accessed 17 June 2022

Chapter 13: Invest responsibly

'Ipsos Mori Issues Index August 2021', Ipsos (August 2021), www.ipsos.com/sites/default/files/ct/news/documents/2021-08/issues-index-august-2021-charts.pdf, accessed on 17 June 2022

Martinez, G, 'Despite outrage, Nike sales increased 31% after Kaepernick ad', *TIME Magazine* (September 2018), https://time.com/5390884/nike-sales-go-up-kaepernick-ad, accessed on 17 June 2022

'Learn about Volkswagen violations', United States Environmental Protection Agency (updated October 2021), www.epa.gov/vw/learn-about-volkswagen-violations, accessed on 17 June 2022

Chapter 14: Your money as a force for good

Broom, D, 'What is sustainable finance and how it is changing the world', WEF (20 January 2022), www.weforum.org/agenda/2022/01/what-is-sustainable-finance, accessed 17 June 2022

'Business Employment Dynamics: Table 7 – Survival of private sector establishments by opening year', Bureau of Labour Statistics (no date), www.bls.gov/bdm/us_age_naics_00_table7.txt, accessed 17 June 2022

'New report shows just 100 companies are source of over 70% of emissions', CDP Network (10 July 2017), www.cdp.net/en/articles/media/new-report-shows-just-100-companies-are-source-of-over-70-of-emissions, accessed 17 June 2022

'Third of UK's biggest companies commit to net zero,' Gov.UK, (30 March 2021), www.gov.uk/government/news/third-of-uks-biggest-companies-commit-to-net-zero, accessed 17 June 2022

Ritchie, H, 'Food production is responsible for one-quarter of the world's greenhouse gas emissions', Our World In Data (November 2019), https://ourworldindata.org/food-ghg-emissions, accessed 17 June 2022

Chapter 15: The crypto conundrum

Bloomberg Crypto Outlook, 'Global Cryptocurrencies 2022 Outlook', Bloomberg (December 2021), https://assets.bbhub.io/professional/sites/10/1489771_Crypto-Dev2021Outlook.pdf, accessed 6 March 2022

Boudette, NE, 'Tesla has first profitable year, but competition is growing', *New York Times* (27 January 2021), www.nytimes.com/2021/01/27/business/tesla-earnings.html, accessed 17 June 2022

'Bitcoin Price Prediction: BTC Forecast', Digitalcoinprice.com (no date), https://digitalcoinprice.com/forecast/bitcoin, accessed September 2022

Dinh, D, 'Crypto Market Report, H1 2022,' Coin98.net, (8 July 2022), www.coin98.net/crypto-market-report-h1-2022, accessed 29 January 2023

Jackson, A, 'Coinbase, Gemini, Binance.US: How 3 of the top crypto brokers compare', MarketWatch, (February 2022), https://www.marketwatch.com/picks/coinbase-gemini-binance-us-how-3-of-the-top-crypto-brokers-compare-01644083457, accessed 17 June 2022

Langton, J, 'Global regulators publish cryptoasset roadmap', InvestmentExecutive.com (7 July 2022), www.investmentexecutive.com/news/from-the-regulators/global-regulators-publish-cryptoasset-roadmap, accessed 29 January 2023

Michael, A, 'What is Cryptocurrency', Forbes.com (July 2022), https://www.forbes.com/uk/advisor/investing/cryptocurrency, accessed 29 January 2023

Ossinger, J, 'Crypto world hits $3 trillion market cap as Ether, Bitcoin Gain', Bloomberg UK (8 November 2021), www.bloomberg.com/news/articles/2021-11-08/crypto-world-hits-3-trillion-market-cap-as-ether-bitcoin-gain, accessed 17 June 2022

Rathi, N, 'How the UK will regulate for the future', FCA.org.uk (14 July 2022), www.fca.org.uk/news/speeches/how-uk-will-regulate-future, accessed 29 January 2023

Rhodes, J, 'Is bitcoin inherently bad for the environment?', Forbes.com (8 October 2021), www.forbes.com/sites/joshuarhodes/2021/10/08/is-bitcoin-inherently-bad-for-the-environment/?sh=37563a333033, accessed 29 January 2023

Schmidt, J and Tetrina, K, 'Top 10 cryptocurrencies in March 2022', Forbes Advisor (Feb 2022)

Sparks, H, 'Infamous bitcoin pizza guy who squandered $365m haul has no regrets', *New York Post* (24 May 2021), https://nypost.com/2021/05/24/bitcoin-pizza-guy-who-squandered-365m-has-no-regrets, accessed 17 June 2022

Chapter 16: Can crypto be good for the planet?

Armstrong, D, Fabiano, A, Rybarczyk, R, 'On Bitcoin's energy consumption: A quantitative approach to a subjective question', Galaxy Digital (May 2021), www.lopp.net/pdf/On_Bitcoin_Energy_Consumption.pdf, accessed 17 June 2022

'Tesla will no longer accept Bitcoin over climate concerns, says Musk,' BBC News (13 May 2021), www.bbc.co.uk/news/business-57096305, accessed 17 June 2022

Beekhuizen, C, 'Ethereum's energy usage will soon decrease by ~99.95%', Ethereum foundation blog (May 2021), https://blog.ethereum.org/2021/05/18/country-power-no-more, accessed on 17 June 2022

'Cambridge Bitcoin Electricity Consumption Index: Comparisons', Cambridge Centre for Alternative Finance (6 March 2022), https://ccaf.io/cbeci/index/comparisons, accessed 17 June 2022

Carroll, M, 'Norway's leading the charge on a sustainable electric future', *National Geographic* (27 June 2019), https://www.nationalgeographic.com/environment/article/partner-content-sustainable-electric-future, accessed on 17 June 2022

'Bitcoin Energy Consumption Index: Energy consumption by country', Digiconomist, (17 June 2022), https://digiconomist.net/bitcoin-energy-consumption, accessed 17 June 2022

'Does Iceland really produce all of its electricity from renewables?' *Iceland Magazine* (15 January 2019), https://icelandmag.is/article/does-iceland-really-produce-all-its-electricity-renewables, accessed 17 June 2022

MacKenzie, S, 'El Salvador's new bitcoin plan could cost money providers like Western Union and others $400 million a year, says President Bukele', CNBC (17 September 2021), www.cnbc.com/2021/09/09/el-salvador-bitcoin-move-could-cost-western-union-400-million-a-year.html, accessed 17 June 2022

Morris, ZM, '1 year of Bitcoin in El Salvador: The bad, the good and the ugly,' Coin Desk (15 September 2022), https://www.coindesk.com/layer2/2022/09/15/one-year-of-bitcoin-in-el-salvador-the-bad-the-good-and-the-ugly/, accessed 29 January 2023

Rhodes, J, 'Is bitcoin inherently bad for the environment?', *Forbes.com* (8 October 2021), www.forbes.com/sites/joshuarhodes/2021/10/08/is-bitcoin-inherently-bad-for-the-environment/?sh=37563a333033, accessed 29 January 2023

Whittam, R, 'Ethereum switches to Proof-of-Stake, will reduce global energy consumption,' Extreme Tech (16 September 2022), https://www.extremetech.com/internet/339592-ethereum-switches-to-proof-of-stake-will-reduce-global-energy-consumption, accessed 17 June 2022

Part Four: Preserve It

Brooks, G, 'Decumulation: The "nastiest, hardest problem in finance"', Embark Group (8 December 2020), https://embarkgroup.co.uk/insights/decumulation-the-nastiest-hardest-problem-in-finance/, accessed 29 January 2023

Chapter 18: How to leave a financial legacy

Gardner, R, *Save Your Acorns*, Lioncrest Publishing, (2016). Available at https://saveyouracorns.com

'Talk, Learn, Do', Money & Pensions Service (2016), https://moneyandpensionsservice.org.uk/talk-learn-do/, accessed 17 June 2022

Acknowledgements

During the summer of 2020, I challenged myself to write a book on the topics I am most passionate about – helping people understand and manage their money and how to build the good habits required to achieve financial freedom in a world worth living in.

I'm very proud of this book, which has come together thanks to the support of the following people.

I want to thank my parents, who instilled good money habits in me, especially during my formative years in Argentina. This gave me a unique insight into the risks of inflation and devaluation of money. In addition, I learned the importance of hard work and saving from them – critical foundations of financial resilience and the first two habits of 'earn it' and 'keep it'. I'd also like to thank them for fact-checking and proof-reading my book every step of the way.

I have been fortunate that my career in finance – from investment banking to pensions and wealth management – has taught me that money can and should be a force for good. Where you earn, spend, save and grow your money can significantly impact the planet's future prosperity and the people living on it. Sharing this message throughout the book has been vital to me.

Setting myself the goal of writing this book was far more challenging than I'd expected, so I'd like to thank Victoria Doxat, my book coach. She helped surface all my ideas and content.

I'd like to thank my publicist and copywriter, Bianca Capstick, for her creative input in rewriting the book and making the financial concepts more relatable and easy to understand.

Thank you to Lauren Smith, whose copywriting skills gave me a fresh perspective on my stories and made the copy more relevant to a younger audience; and to Alexandra Loydon and Ed Gascoigne for technical proofreading of the book at the final stage.

Special thanks go to Carl Richards, who has brought my book to life with his brilliant illustrations. Making money concepts relatable is vital for me, and Carl's illustrations are an excellent visual summary of each chapter's key message.

Several friends and colleagues took the time to review one or more drafts of this book. What has amazed me is the divergence of opinion and perspective, and I am grateful for each comment and insight, all of which have helped enormously in shaping the book. I wanted to thank Susie Ashfield, Lucy Clark, Raheem Mirza, Annette Morgan and Miriam Murphy.

Thank you to my editors and Rethink Press for their meticulous care in getting the book ready to be published.

Last but not least, I want to thank my wife, Sanaz, and my children, Tara and Camilla. They have supported me unconditionally in finding the time to write this book. The financial freedom of my daughters, and the world they grow up in, is a crucial driver to my ambition to make money a force for good.

The Author

 Robert Gardner is a money expert, entrepreneur and financial activist on a mission to make money a force for good for people and the planet, to create 'financial wellbeing in a world worth living in'.

As a father of two, Rob understands the importance of financial education and long-term financial freedom. His life's work has been to make money relatable and easy to understand, helping empower financial literacy in everyone from primary school children to pensioners.

In 2012 Rob co-founded RedSTART, a financial education charity which aims to plant the seeds for the financial freedom of young people. In 2016 he wrote the children's book *Save Your Acorns* to help make conversations about money an ongoing part of family life. In addition, he has delivered a TEDx talk on financial education among young people titled, 'If You Leave Your Children One Thing, Make It This. . .' He is regularly asked to speak about making money a force for good, having appeared on, or been invited to comment in, BBC Radio, *Daily Mail*, *Daily Mirror*, *Good Housekeeping* magazine, *The Financial Times*, Sky News, *The Times* and more.

In 2006, Rob shook up the UK's pensions market with the launch of Redington, now a leading investment consultancy whose mission is to create financial well-being for 100 million people in a way that protects the planet's future. Having studied Geography at the University of Oxford, Rob's love of glaciers and passion for the planet's prosperity have heavily influenced his role in financial services. Responsible investment and using his position and expertise to drive better businesses for the earth and its people was a crucial part of his previous role as St. James's Place's (SJP) Director of Investments. In addition, Rob was a member of the World Economic Forum and sat on their retirement council.

Rob is now a co-founder of Rebalance Earth, whose goal is to make money a force for good to help reverse

climate change and biodiversity loss. By creating
high-integrity biodiversity credits, that puts a mon-
etary value on nature based on its ability to absorb
carbon, protect and grow biodiversity, and support
local communities that preserve it. Companies buy
these credits as the most effective, quick and verifiable
way of being nature positive and achieving net-zero.

in Robert Gardner

🐦 @Robertjgardner

📷 @Robertjgardner

Printed in Great Britain
by Amazon

36374505R00148